Female Emancipation, Male Voices in Colonial India

Unity is meaningless without the accompaniment of women. Education is fruitless without educated women, and agitation is incomplete without the strength of women.

Dr. B.R. Ambedkar

Published by
Prestige Books International
New Delhi 110 060
prestigebooks@gmail.com
Phone: 9818755529

Associate Office
P.O. Box 2250
Sydney 2001
Australia

ISBN: 978-81-956029-1-9

Printed in India

Female Emancipation, Male Voices in Colonial India

Raja Rammohun Roy | **Mahatma Jyotirao Phule**
Mahatma Gandhi | **Dr. B.R. Ambedkar**

K. Karuna Devi

Prestige Books International
New Delhi

Contents

Dedicated

to

My Parents

Foreword

Gender and its ramifications have occupied human thought from times immemorial. Gendered narratives, gender typing, gender conditioning, attempts at gender neutrality and gender parity continue to be foregrounded in a variety of narratives even today. And in all this the role and position of women has occupied centre-stage.

Going back to the hoary past of India, one can observe a different picture of women in the public sphere—a more equitable balance between men and women than later. This even tenor was gradually obliterated and the thousand years of colonization of the country have had a very sizeable impact on this fall of women's position—with special emphasis on the two centuries of British colonization.

Obviously, one of the forms of protest offering correctives to the social ills of the times took the shape of bringing women to those spheres of influence from which they had hitherto been kept away. The forward-looking men who realized the need for this and who raised their voices to effect a change did much to improve the situation of women in the colonized nation. These voices were the pioneers of a task which is continuing even at present. Parallels to this can be found in global writings and strivings.

Dr. Karuna Devi has made some very relevant and insightful observations about all these aspects in this volume significantly titled *Female Emancipation, Male Voices in Colonial India*. For her research she has chosen four influential male voices: Raja Rammohun Roy, Mahatma Jyotirao Phule, Mahatma Gandhi and Dr. B.R. Ambedkar. As she rightly says about her volume, "The aim is to critically evaluate the variety of discourses used by them." A list of numerous reformers who have contributed to this field is mentioned and these can serve as keys to further research. For her work the researcher has chosen only four as this appears to be a manageable canvas for the scope of the study.

Each of the four has made a unique contribution and all four together provide a complementary image. Roy was the one who introduced a new thought process to change the mindset of people about women. A personal tragedy was the impetus for his involvement in 'female emancipation'. Phule practiced what he preached and this is evident in the way he involved and gave a leadership role to his own wife in his attempt to bring education to women. Gandhi encouraged women to come out of their sheltered lives in the cloister of their home and take up *satyagraha* from the front-lines. Ambedkar brought in his legal expertise to critique the existing state of women and suggested possibilities for betterment.

All the four thinkers chosen for study have, thus, taken up different aspects pertaining to 'female emancipation' and have left behind them some very remarkable results. Their writings serve as a foundation for much of the ongoing work in this field.

This volume has a wide sweep and depth in dealing with the crucial human endeavor of ensuring the deserved rights to women. By reviewing the opinions of the 'male voices' being studied here, we can see how the process of bringing in gender justice is introduced. Essential in strengthening the social fabric, of which women form about half the number, is a crucial task. Therefore, such research needs to be encouraged and the findings widely disseminated.

My best wishes to the author and happy reading to all.

Sumita Roy

Professor Sumita Roy

Acknowledgements

The present book is the by-product of my interest in the literature of Colonial India, especially in the discourses which contributed to the emancipatory movement for the liberation of women in India.

In all that concerns this book, I express my deepest gratitude to my mentor, emblematic role model Professor Sumita Roy, (Retd.) Head, Department of English, Osmania University, for her scholarly suggestions and invaluable guidance.

I am grateful to Dr. R.K. Dhawan and Dr. Suman Bala from University of Delhi who gave me editorial advice from time to time and also helped me in getting the book published so expeditiously and elegantly.

I would like to thank the staff of the libraries of Andhra Mahila Sabha Arts and Science College for Women, for preserving many rare books which were helpful to me, especially books on Raja Rammohun Roy and Mahatma Gandhi. I also thank the staff of English and Foreign Languages University Library, British Council Library and Osmania University Library—all in Hyderabad.

I express my deepest gratitude to my father, Sri Tatyarao Kamble, who has always been a source of lively debates on various wider issues and generous in sharing ideas, greatly improving my understanding of the history of ideas. This has immensely helped me in my research work. And to my mother, Smt. Nirmala Kamble, who is the pillar of my strength. And to my mother-in-law, late Smt. Lakshmi Bai Dange, who despite being illiterate, always supported me with her liberal thoughts. Heartfelt thanks to my husband, Dr. Tippanna Dange, for being with me at every step in all my endeavours. I am grateful to my siblings, my sister Nalanda Kamble, and my brothers Dr. Pradnya Kamble and Mr. Milind Kamble for their support in all walks of life. And to my sister-in-law Mrs. Maheshwari Kamble for her support. Last but not the least, I adore my nephew Samrat Kamble who injects energy in me with his love.

Hyderabad **K. Karuna Devi**

Introduction

The phrase 'Women's empowerment' in the vocabulary of gender literature is used in two broad senses—general and specific. In a general sense, it refers to empowering women to be self-dependent by providing them access to all the freedom and opportunities denied to them in the past by virtue of their gender. In a specific sense, women's empowerment refers to enhancing the position of women in the power structure of society. Women's empowerment essentially means that women have the power / capacity to regulate their day-to-day lives in social, political and economic terms—a power which enables them to move from the periphery to the center stage.

To achieve the present status women in India have traveled a great distance over the past few centuries. From ancient to modern times, the position of women in India has seen many crests and troughs. In the recent past, the most eventful period was the nineteenth century which created a new India with liberalism as one of the basic principles. This liberalism prepared the masses to accept, in principle, the emancipation of the Indian woman from her limited sphere of action.

The present book is a study of the works of selected reformers pertaining to 'female emancipation'. The aim is to critically evaluate the variety of discourses used by them. Female emancipation became a necessity at a time when India was also fighting for its emancipation from British rule. The male voices who were striving for political emancipation from the British Empire were also involved in this parallel movement of emancipation of women. The impact of Western thought and the introduction of English in India were significant events which impelled the reformers to be innovative. This they did by merging the occidental and oriental ideologies especially with relation to rethinking the roles and responsibilities of women.

This book is divided into six chapters: the first chapter is the introduction, highlighting the background of the status of women in India and giving a brief history of Indian women in the nineteenth century, with the focus on male voices and their discourses which contributed to the movement of bringing freedom to women. Chapters two, three, four and five focus on the respective reformers' works along with their brief biographies to place them in context. The sixth chapter contains a critique on the discourses used by the selected reformers and the conclusions formed on the basis of the analysis in the earlier chapters.

The study is limited to only one section of the society, namely Hindus. This is because the subject of women's emancipation is very vast when encompassing all religious groups available in India. In order to give my study a sharper focus, the area of analysis has been limited. Also, in spite of India being multi-cultural and multi-religious, the background of the people belonging to different religions is common. They follow a common culture, especially with regard to issues relating to the question of women which are more or less the same across India. Therefore, instead of being a limiting factor, the analysis of this one section serves as a case study applicable to others with minor alterations.

Before beginning this study, it is relevant to direct our attention towards a brief history of women in India with special emphasis on changes in their status over a period of time. There is also a need to examine the efforts towards emancipation of women by educated Indian men with liberal ideas. The colonial era brought new thought currents into the minds of the Indian intelligentsia and also a new mode of expression—that is, English. These were the tools used by the reformers chosen for study. Using them, these visionary men expressed their convictions about the emancipation of women in a variety of discourses.

In the course of recent Indian history women generally have had fewer legal rights and career opportunities than men. Wifehood and motherhood were regarded as women's most significant contributions. In the twentieth century, however, women in most nations won the right to vote and got some opportunities for education and jobs. Perhaps most importantly, they fought for and accomplished to a large extent, a re-evaluation of traditional views of their roles in society.

But ancient Indian history tells a different tale. India was a pioneer among nations where the attitude toward women was favorable. In ancient India, women were not deprived of property rights or individual preference in choosing a partner for marriage. But as Hinduism evolved in India after about 500 BC, gender became the determining factor for assigning the sphere of activity. Many restrictions were imposed on women. For example, women had to walk behind their husbands; they could not own property and widows could not remarry; male children were preferred over female children.

Gender discrimination was not necessarily an Indian malady. Some of the so-called progressive societies were also bogged down by it. For instance, by the end of the eighteenth century in America, individual liberty based on gender was being hotly debated. In 1789, during the French Revolution, Olympe de Gouges published a *Declaration of the Rights of Woman* to protest against the revolutionists' failure to mention women in their *Declaration of the Rights of Man*. In *A Vindication of the Rights of Women* (1792) Mary Wollstonecraft called for enlightenment of the female mind. Margaret Fuller, one of the earliest female reporters, in *Woman in the Nineteenth Century* (1845) argued that individuals had unlimited capacities and that when people's roles were defined according to their gender, human development was severely limited. Elizabeth Cady Stanton, a leading theoretician of the women's rights movement, in *Woman's Bible*, (published in parts in 1895 and 1898) attacked what she called the male bias of the Bible.

During the early twentieth century women's emancipation was a global issue; the term 'new woman' came to be used in the popular press. More young women than ever before started going to schools, working both in blue-and white-collar jobs, and living by themselves in city apartments. These changes in attitudes and patterns of behavior came under the broad rubric of feminism. Some social critics feared that feminism, which they interpreted to mean the end of the home and family, was triumphing. Actually, the customary habits of American women were changing little. Although young people dated more than their parents did and used the automobile to escape parental supervision, most young women still married and became the traditional housewives and mothers.

Women in the United States during the nineteenth century organized and participated in a variety of reform movements to improve education, to initiate prison reform, to ban alcoholic drinks, and, during the pre-Civil War period, to free the slaves. Some women saw parallels between the position of women and that of the slaves. In their view, both were expected to be passive, cooperative, and obedient to their master-husbands. Women such as Lucy Stone, Lucretia Mott, Harriet Tubman, and Sojourner Truth were feminists and abolitionists, believing in both the rights of women and the rights of blacks. Many women supported the temperance movement in the belief that drunken husbands pulled their families into poverty. In 1872 the Prohibition Party became the first national political party to recognize the right of suffrage for women.

A striking contrast manifested itself in Indian society. At a time when the women of other nations were fighting for their rights on their own, the Indian women were not even aware of the inhuman treatment meted out to them. On the contrary, they followed all the traditions without questioning or reasoning. Though in India women have been worshipped and honoured in the Vedas and mythologies, there were times when women were subjected to bondage and sufferance by way of inhuman restrictions and customs like the dowry system, child marriage, *sati*, *devadasi* system, forced polygamy imposed on them by the men in Indian society. It was a critical context which called for radical measures and one can take it as India's unique contribution to the gender issues that it was male voices which tried to bring women their human rights. Reformers such as Raja Rammohun Roy, Mahatma Jyoti Rao Phule, Mahatma Gandhi and Dr. B.R. Ambedkar articulated the dismal condition of women and ways to mitigate this evil.

They were undeterred by the aggressive reactions of the people around them. The methodology used in the present book is to explore how the tools of textual analysis can be employed to reveal gaps and contradictions in a narrative of events which is otherwise taken for granted as simply representing a world of coherent and continuous reality. In the process of textual analysis, the theories and approaches suggested by some theorists on discourse analyses like Michel Foucault, Louise Phillips, Marianne W Jorgensen, Norman Fairclough, Terry Locke, David Howarth, Jan Blommaert, will also be used selectively. Discourse is a vast subject in language studies but here we only need to use those aspects of it which help to analyze the expression/ thought of the reformers on how to improve the conditions of the women of India.

Before exploring the discourses of reformers it is essential to survey the history of gender equations in India. Some scholars are of the belief that in the earlier Vedic period women enjoyed equal status on par with men in all spheres of life. A particular mention is made about women in the tenth chapter of the Rig Veda in order to emphasize the position and status of women in Vedic times, extolling her as the Empress of the Universe, the Fulfiller of all Prayers. During the last phase of the Vedic period, also we find women enjoying a status on par with men.

However, the position and the status of women gradually began to decline with the ascendancy of Manu, the chief Hindu law codifier, who curtailed women's freedom and rights, totally upsetting their position and status in the house, society and religion. During the period of Manu, probably between 200 B.C and A.D. 200, women were condemned in several passages of the sacred books wherein the complete dependence of a woman on others for her identity from her birth was glaringly mentioned. Manu categorically asserted that a woman should depend on her father till her marriage, on her husband after the marriage and on her son after the death of her husband. Such injunctions were the bases of controversy relating to the significance and sphere of influence enjoyed by women—a debate which has been ongoing for centuries now.

A look at post-independent India reveals that the freedom and the rights of women continue to remain a perennial subject of discussion even today among diverse groups: sociologists, philosophers, politicians, social reformers and religious monks. Since the growth and development of society depends equally on the progress and development of women as of men, women's emancipation is a topical issue in all societies engaging its best minds. Much has been said and written about women's education and their consciousness of various social and political issues of today which provide them with a platform of their own to fight for their right of equality in education, employment and politics. The rights of women were not only recognized as an inseparable chapter of human rights as enshrined in the Indian constitution under the nomenclature of "Fundamental Rights" but also their empowerment was recognized as one of the main policies of the political programme of each political party aspiring to win the Assembly and Parliamentary elections. As a result, the year 2001 was officially declared as 'the Year of the Women's Empowerment' by the Government of India.

Obviously, such concerted efforts brought about the desired changes in the status of women. Today women have the opportunity to excel in all fields. They can actively participate in various movements and campaigns for constructive actions like, river revival programmes, rain water harvesting, watershed management scheme, abolition of belt shops, issues relating to Right to Information Act, etc. The election of almost one million women to Panchayat Raj bodies and their activities in other elected bodies has brought about a strategic shift in many of the developmental activities at the grassroots level. From the private sphere of existence women have thus graduated to the public sphere of influence.

While women's involvement and active participation in the world outside the 'home and hearth' is gaining momentum, the ill-treatment meted out to them and atrocities against them has not abated. Not a single day passes without news in print and electronic media or T.V. channels item reporting incidents of atrocities against and killing of women. In the modern times, Indian women have been given rights such as freedom of expression and equality as well as the right to education. But even today, we are fighting against social evils such as dowry, female infanticide, sex selective abortions, domestic violence, etc.

The dowry system is not only responsible for snuffing out the lives of innocent women at a very young age but is also equally the single most important cause for the growing incidence of female feticide in our country. Incidences of rape, domestic violence, sexual harassment at work places and trafficking of women have increased by leaps and bounds. More than half of the women killed in India today are killed in their bedrooms. No place is safe for them, not even their mother's womb as they are put to death even before they are born. The former President of India, KR. Narayanan, addressing the nation on 25 January 2002, had expressed his deep concern over the issue of women's emancipation: "The problems of women in India today represent the problems of inequalities and injustices in society in general. Even today it is shocking that women have not become an *inclusive society* in spite of India being the world's largest democracy." (Paradeshi 43)

The conclusion is obvious: emancipation is on the surface and often restricted to a small percentage of women while the majority still exist on the margins and their status is on a gradual decline in spite of various upliftment projects and programmes. What began in the medieval period has not been arrested even today. Chapters of history bear mute witness to this fact. For instance, the Muslim conquerors in the Indian subcontinent brought the *purdah* system into Indian society. Among the Rajputs of Rajasthan *jauhar* was practiced. In some parts of India, the *devadasi* or the women dedicated to the temples were sexually exploited. Polygamy was widely practiced especially among the Hindu Kshatriya rulers.

Into this stark picture of reality, the contribution of the four reformers chosen for study in this book can be foregrounded from two major perspectives: social critique and attempts at resolution of gender discrepancies. In their critique of the society which fostered their thoughts, these reformers took up issues such as *Sati*, *jauhar*, *purdah*, child marriage and *devadasi* that were imposed upon women as a part of Hindu traditions.

And in their attempts at resolution they used both their writings and their activities to root out some unsavory customs. For instance, s*ati* was a social custom which became gradually defunct at the instance of social reformers like Raja Rammohun Roy and by the British Law enacted during 1829. According to this custom, on the death of her husband a woman was required to immolate herself alive by sitting at the feet of her dead husband on the funeral pyre. What began as a voluntary custom for women became a compulsion later and it was forced upon those women who were reluctant to follow this practice. It's inhuman enforcement on Raja Rammohun Roy's sister-in-law when his brother died had deeply shocked Roy who subsequently and successfully fought for its abolition. Even after independence, forty cases of *sati* were reported. The Roop Kanwar case of *sati* in the state of Rajasthan led to the commission of *sati* (prevention) Act 1987. This practice was mostly prevalent among the families of the kshatriya, Brahmin and other upper Hindu castes.

Jauhar was another painful yet glorified custom that was in vogue in Rajasthan. This custom was prevalent among the Rajputs of the Rajasthan state. During wars between kings, whenever one king was defeated and taken as captive or killed by the victorious king, the wives and the daughters of the vanquished king would resort to voluntary immolation in order to avoid forceful capture and imminent molestation by the enemy and to protect their honour and dignity.

Child marriages were another inhuman practice. In olden days, young girls, even below the age of puberty, were married to old men in spite of their physical and mental immaturity. Soon after their marriage, as the old men died, the young girls had to lead the life of a widow, suppressing their physical desires and mental pleasures. They were condemned to a life of great mental agony as they were forced to live in isolation with shaved heads, shunned by the society. Though child marriages were abolished in 1860, this inhuman practice still prevails in some parts of the country.

The practice of *devadasi* was a symbol of male dominance that prevailed in some parts of southern India. According to this custom, women were married to a deity or a temple only to be sexually exploited by men of a feudalistic background.

All these customs led to a situation where women were subjected to oppression and tyranny which called for curative action in the form of emancipation that would include the restoration of equal social rights on par with men in society.

The awareness created by social reformers influenced the general perception about practices and moral conduct, and *sastric* injections. In fact, social reformers have different interpretations to *sastric* injections, and this had a salutary effect on society. Women were made to understand the inherent possibilities of looking at structure and patterns of life in an innovative manner which could find sanction in the *smritis* as well as the rhythms of their present life. With such an altered awareness, a number of women broke away from the traditional life patterns to take advantage of the new possibilities and opportunities. In this way, a beginning was made in the nineteenth century for the emancipation of women from social bondages to bring about equality.

Till the first decade of the twentieth century, social reforms in India were increasingly scattered and fragmented into regional ambits, becoming part of the emerging regional identities like Raja Rammohun Roy and Jyotirao Phule. Later, Dr. Ambedkar took up the issue of social reform at the all-India level once again and in a way made Gandhi accord priority to it.

Raja Rammohun Roy denounced the custom of *sati* and tried to prove that none of the Hindu prescriptive texts laid down that a widow must commit *sati*; in effect, its incidence testified to the degeneration of Hindu ethos. When the orthodox Hindus argued that *sati* was a means to achieve virtuous knowledge and a gift to their families, Raja Rammohun Roy retorted: "The women clearly possessed virtuous knowledge, for their lives were 'infinitely more self-sacrificing than men'." (Gosh 363)

Gandhi appealed to women of India to enter the struggle for India's freedom. He wrote in *Young India* dated 10 April 1930, that "if non-violence is the law of our being, the future is with women'.(Joshi 222) As far back as 1921, after the conclusion of the Benares Congress session, Gandhi wrote that 'women of India should have as much share in winning *Swaraj* as men. Probably in this peaceful struggle women cannot distance men by many a mile. I hope that the women all over India will take-up the challenge and organize themselves'. The Gandhian era gave Indian women an opportunity to enter nationalist politics. Here, more emphasis is laid on the word 'emancipation' because in the nineteenth century women had no say in social issues. Therefore, liberating them from religious, legal, economic, and sexual oppression was the need of the hour and so was their access to higher education.

This study perceives 'emancipation' as a movement, a discourse for the rights of women. In simple terms, it is a belief in the social, political and economic equality of the sexes, and a movement organized around the conviction that biological sex should not be the pre-determining factor for shaping a person's social identity or socio-political or economic rights. The importance of educating women was first discussed publicly in Bengal by the Arya Sabha, founded by Rammohun Roy in 1815.

The expression '*Male Voices*' used in the title of this book also requires a critical comment as much as does 'female emancipation'. It is because women could not raise their voice because of their subordination that men had to be their mouthpiece. They could not protest against various evil-practices in society, as discussed above. Women did not have any independence and they were kept away from education. They were kept under complete control through myths and superstitions. Another significant reason for the predominance of male voices in the emancipation of women is that men of courage, erudition and values were already in the Indian struggle for freedom and their fight was an epic fight of heroic dimensions. For example Dr. Ambedkar advocated that women's rights should not be dismissed on the grounds of culture, family, or religion and that the rights of all to dignity and freedom from violence, in all its forms must be respected; this included both the citizens of a colonial nation as well as women in a patriarchal society.

There were many social reformers like Eshwar Chand Vidyasagar, Swami Dayanand Saraswati, Kandukuri Veeresalingam Pantalu, M.G. Ranade and many others, who contributed significantly to the cause of women. But to fit into the canvas of a book only four reformers: Raja Rammohun Roy, Jyotirao Phule, Mohandas Karamchand Gandhi and Dr. Bheem Rao Ambedkar were selected. They represent some of the most effective voices contributing to the women's cause, as has been widely acknowledged and recognized by the people of India. Each of their unique contributions as pioneers serves as a turning point in the emancipatory movement of women. Raja Rammohun Roy dared to face the orthodox people of his community by questioning the very practice of *sati* and laid the foundation for the Indian renaissance. He was the first Hindu who not only severely condemned this practice but also made emphatic public protest challenging its validity by quoting relevant scriptures. Phule challenged the very edifice of Hindu philosophy (scriptures) and the proponents of religion by opening schools—the channels of education for the most condemned untouchable women of the time. Phule's induction of the women into the flood gate of knowledge was a shock to the orthodox Hindus and a turning point in the women's movement. It not only made the women of higher caste more conscious of disparities but also changed the very mindset of men towards women. When Gandhi joined the Indian freedom movement, he gave an opportunity to women to come out of their private domain and play a greater role in national politics thus boosting their morale. He was successful in bringing ordinary women into the freedom struggle. The pioneering effort of Dr Ambedkar to liberate the Hindu women from the clutches of the religiously managed patriarchal society through legislative and constitutional measures gave a major fillip to the very attitude towards women's rights in the pre-independent era. Though these reformers came from different strata of the society, their understanding of the plight of women was sensitive. At a time when women were subjected to all sorts of humiliation as a matter of right, these pioneers dared to take up the cause of women overcoming almost insurmountable odds.

Even in postcolonial India, women's issues demand attention. Hence mention can again be made of Dr. Ambedkar, who, through the various clauses of the Indian Constitution, aimed to promote change in social and economic structures so that complete equality for women, greater participation of women in the development process and national strategies without discrimination, and, constitutional and legislative guarantee of the principle of non-discrimination, and equal opportunities in education and work were achieved. Women's emancipation leading to empowerment with the legislations brought in through the vision of Ambedkar. He codified what was needed for the society and rejected all that was against the principles of liberty, equality and natural justice. Ambedkar's attempt to awaken the society for more than six decades can be treated as a landmark in the annals of Indian women's movement towards empowerment.

The struggle for equality has a long history and is likely to continue. In traditionally patriarchal societies any improvement in the status of women has far-reaching consequences and produces fundamental political changes. Therefore, it is always resisted by the established patriarchal power structures. However, it seems certain that the patriarchal power structures will ultimately have to relent, because the emancipation of women is both necessary and desirable. It will bring about a greater degree of social justice and thus benefit everyone. Some of the representatives of patriarchy were reformers and other revolutionaries, but virtually all of them worked for a better, more equitable and more humane world. Much can be learnt from their experiences. They often suffered ridicule, persecution and defeat, but also won admiration, support, and victory. Gradually, they achieved their goals. Their opponents, on the other hand, learned that a just cause cannot be suppressed forever. Whenever reforms are consistently blocked, revolution becomes inevitable.

Moving on from here to the word 'Colonial' in the title of the desertion, we can begin by a definition of the term. Colonial means "relating to a country that controls and rules other countries, usually ones that are far away", it also means "someone who lives in a colony but who is a citizen of the country that rules the colony". India's colonial history is inextricably linked with the male voices discoursing on women's emancipation—this is the basic premise on which the present study is based.

An absorbing variety of British attitudes towards India accompanied the formation of this empire. From the time of Edmund Burke until John Stuart Mill, a host of Britons came in contact with India. They were from all ranks and intellectual levels—soldiers, officials, political leaders, merchants, missionaries, historians, poets and philosophers. They were confronted with a strange and distant land, whose people and social conditions, political and economic practices, art, religions and learning were quite different from anything in Britain. They left behind an astonishingly large record of their reactions to India as evidence of some significant British attitudes to India.

The contrast between Britain and India during the period was striking. Britain was a growing nation in possession of the techniques, organization, and energy which would enable her to become a world power. She was in the midst of a political, social and economic transformation. George Bearce has rightly referred to Emery Neff, a historian, in describing Britain from 1760 onwards: "By 1840 Britain was far losing her medieval aspect and becoming very like the England of today." (Bearce 3-4)

Britain's transformation from a rural, aristocratic, conservative society to an industrialized, modern nation was of great importance to the development of British attitudes towards India. This social and economic change had its effect. Britain now had the power necessary for imperial greatness. It also had a society which demanded sweeping changes and which was impatient with the old order of things.

The establishment of the East India Company in India in the early nineteenth century ushered in a new era in India. The advent of British Rule in India through the East India Company paved the way for the birth of modern India. In spite of political subjugation, it brought development in the fields of education, trade and commerce, transport and communication, law and rule of jurisprudence. At the same time, a new spark of Indian nationalism was set off in the minds of Indians and the British colonial rule was mainly responsible for generating a sense of nationalism among Indians.

During colonial rule, Indian society was pluralistic in form and character. It was divided by medieval culture and feudalistic forces. India was largely caste-ridden and therefore lacked a strong and unified political and economic base. The vastness of its geographical territory inhabited by a large population speaking languages of perplexing multiplicity, professing different religions and following diverse cultures posed a serious challenge to the British colonial rule.

As a result, the immediate aim of the British rulers was to have complete control over the land and its people. The British rulers were basically conquerors and not reformers. Their main objective was to consolidate their gains in India without any resistance from Indians. Once they conquered considerable portions of the Indian territory, the achievement of their objective was complete. Conquest and consolidation went hand in hand in their case. During their initial rule, they adopted a very cautious approach in so far as the social and religious problems were concerned. Hence Indian society during the earlier phase of the British rule retained the same form as it had had before the advent of the British colonial rule.

Hinduism, which was the main religion of over two thirds of the population with its castes and subcastes, posed a serious challenge in the process of unification of India politically, socially and economically. The Hindu religion itself was not homogeneous. Its heterogeneous nature could be seen in its conglomeration of diverse religious cults leading to serious repercussions for political and social cohesion. Moreover, the divisive character of Hindu religion had created a number of problems in society such as the divide between the rich and the poor, the high and the low, the pure and the impure and the chaste and the unchaste leading to serious social divisions and differences which continued to be preserved for centuries. The age-old religious customs, social practices and individual attitudes were opposed to the democratic principles of individual liberty, social equality and economic independence.

Colonial rule created an extremely delicate psycho-cultural situation for the Indians. While presenting her views on Colonialism and its implications for Indians, Gail Omvedt wrote:

> Colonialism for India meant a political organization that shaped the traditional caste-feudal structures and Mughal bureaucracies to the needs of a new British-controlled colonial state; a restructuring of 'local production processes' that meant an increased 'peasantization' as many traditional crafts were destroyed and peasants thrown back on the land, often to specialization in crops not for their own sustenance or local consumption but for the needs of Europe; and an accumulation process that directed surpluses to countries far from India itself but also helped to strengthen the political bureaucracy within India. In this process the traditional structures of caste were used, transformed and in some way even strengthened. (83)

Obviously, every Indian was a victim to these pressures but the situation was perhaps more intense for intellectuals who learnt English and came into immediate contact with the British and consequently with ideology in all its debilitating detail. Confronted with the ideology of colonialism, Indian intellectuals reacted in two ways. At a public level, they plunged into the reformation of their religion, customs, and their people with a zeal that surpassed that of the British liberals. On the other hand, they felt constrained, at a personal level, to prove their humanity in the eyes of those who doubted it. It was necessary for them to demonstrate that Indians were not innately or naturally bestial just as their customs and beliefs were not innately depraved and that with stern application one could attain an intellectual ability as well as strength of character and purpose that was on par with that of the white man. While analyzing the role of English educated Indians, Rajshekhariah observes: "It was realized by the Indian intelligentsia who came to be imbued with liberal ideas under the impact of western education that unless these religious superstitions were eradicated from the minds of our people, Indian socialism could not be firmly rooted on Indian soil. Hence, came a number of movements in the later part of the nineteenth century." (4)

The result of this attitude was that many evil customs entailed upon women continued and even flourished under the garb of Hinduism. The British colonialists were mainly concerned with the question of maintenance of law and order and of tracking such social evils which were, in the main, social injustices that might disturb peace and order. Their attitude as administrators was mainly one of neutralism, which they had believed was expected of them, if they wanted to dispense equity amongst the various cultural ethnic groups that made India a pluralistic society. To the British rulers such things as untouchability and caste had flourished in India since times immemorial and would continue to exist. It was no use trying to remove them. Indeed, in the eyes of diehards, the continued existence of such abuses provided an excellent excuse for the indefinite continuance of British rule in India. But such an attitude could not be maintained for long. They were suspected due to their innate fear that they might bring Christianity through their flag. They were suspected of getting involved in local religious wrangles which might negate their political influence. They also strongly felt that their involvement might invite the wrath and the hostility of the Hindu religious leaders, if they began tinkering with social reformers as they were based on rigorous religious sanctions.

Dr. Ambedkar referred to this attitude of the British Government in India while speaking at the plenary session of the First Round Table Conference and accused the Government of utter negligence of the problem of social change in general, and of untouchability in particular. Dr. Ambedkar said:

> The British Government has accepted the social arrangement as it found them and has preserved them faithfully . . . our wrongs have

> remained as open sores and they have not been righted, although 150 years of British Government in India suffers from two very serious limitations. There is first of all an internal limitation, which prevents them from appreciating the living forces operating in our society, makes them indifferent and inimical to its aspirations and apathetic to our education. It is not because they cannot help us in these things but because it is against their character, motives and interest to do so. The second consideration that limits its authority is the moral fear it has of external resistance. (Rajshekhariah 21)

The net effect of such an attitude of neutralism on the part of the British was disastrous as testified by Brailsford:

> Nonetheless, our official policy was then, as now, to interfere as little as possible with Indian institutions: it tolerated social customs injurious to health, social order, notably child marriages, and accepted even untouchability as an immutable fact in an environment it dare not alter. Our courts, as time went on, took to administering Hindu law with an almost antiquarian fidelity. The result of this attitude was unquestionably to stereotype the past in a land that never has discarded it with ease. (21)

Besides the clash and conflict found in the relations of British and India, a peaceful, often mutually advantageous contact occurred between the two countries. Britons and Indians recognized the great differences between them, and many of them tried to bridge this gap. Britons such as Sir William Jones, a scholar of oriental literature and languages, tried to introduce an understanding of Indian culture into Europe. Indians such as Raja Rammohun Roy became students of western science and philosophy and sought to encourage an Indian understanding of western ideas and institutions. Such mutually advantageous contact, British appreciation of Indian society and culture and Indian respect for and acquiescence to British rule, made the British Empire in India possible. In this context, David Hume observed: "As a force is always on the side of the governed, the governors have nothing to support them but opinion." (Bearce 7)

Colonialism, thus, had a complex effect on the functioning of various Indian customs such as the caste system. It did not simply create 'classes' along with 'caste'. On the one hand, new groups like a factory working class and plantation proletariat came into existence. On the other hand, new professions and businesses made brahmins and baniyas the pillars of high caste Hindu society. Peasantry also acquired an accentuated existence, increasingly linked to production for the world market. But while at one level formally non-scriptive opening such as education and entry into factory occupation could mean that very few from the lower caste channeled workers to the segmented labour markets. The conditions maintained a status quoin the existing social customs and religious practices especially pertaining to women which continued unchanged. Consequently female emancipation from these evils gradually gained momentum over a period of time till it was vigorously taken up by the social reformers mentioned earlier.

It is significant to note that during the nineteenth century European scholars particularly noticed that the Hindu women were "naturally chaste" and "more virtuous" than women of many other nations. It was the highest tribute that they could have paid to Indian women. But the same virtuous women, though regarded as virtuous and chaste, needed social emancipation as they were enslaved socially and religiously. Women's emancipation was, therefore, the need of the hour. During the colonial period, many reformers such as Raja Rammohun Roy, Eswar Chandra Vidya Sagar and Jyotirao Phule, fought for the cause of women through their speeches and writings. Raja Rammohun Roy's efforts led to the abolition of the evil practice of *sati* in 1829. Eshwar Chandra Vidya Sagar's powerful crusade for the upliftment of the widows paved a way to the Widow Remarriage Act of 1856.

Most reformers stressed the need for educating women first. Thus, a few women came forward and started getting educated. These efforts yielded fruit later when even women reformers such as Pandita Ramabai worked for the cause of women's upliftment.

In 1917 the first women's delegation met the Secretary of State to demand political rights for women as supported by the Indian National Congress. The All-India Women's Education Conference which was held in Pune in 1927 was instrumental in getting the Child Marriage Restraint Act passed stipulating fourteen years as the minimum age for the marriage of girls, which has been increased to 18 years now. Though Mahatma Gandhi was married at the age of thirteen, he subsequently exhorted the people to boycott child marriage and called upon young men to consider child widows also as prospective brides for themselves.

Through their strong championship of women the reformers drew women who were confined to their homes into the outer world. Women started coming out to participate in hitherto male-dominated fields of activity and play an important role in society. This could be seen in the important roles women played in India's struggle for independence. Some of the famous women freedom fighters included Annie Beasant, Pritilata Waddedar, Vijaya Laxmi Pandit, Rajkumari Amrit Kaur, Anjali Ammal, Aruna Asaf Ali, Suchetha Kriplani, Sarojini Naidu, Durgabai Deshmukh. Sarojini Naidu, a reputed poet and freedom fighter, was the first Indian woman to become the president of the Indian National Congress and also the first woman to become the Governor of a state in independent India.

All these were part of the positive effects of colonization. O'Malley has rightly pointed out the positive change brought about the western impact on Indian minds in the following words: "The impact of the West on Indian civilization has brought about changes that are more fundamental in the case of women than men. To men it brought a new conception of the world, of its material resources, ethical standards and political possibilities, but to women it brought slowly but potentially a new conception of themselves. If men re-assessed themselves as citizens in a new India, women revalued themselves as human beings in a new social order." (448)

In addition to the women's angle, colonization also gave Indians a new language and discourse for self-expression. The reformers chosen for study here make use of English in a particular way and this is the framework within which their writings will be analyzed. Here the term 'discourse' used in the title of the book comes into play. Discourse in this study means "the language used in a particular type of speech or writing". Each of the four thinkers have used a distinct discourse to communicate his ideology. There are some similarities and a variety of differences in their individual discourse which has a sizable impact on whatever they wrote or spoke about.

"Discourse", which is diversely used in social, political, religious and philosophical context, is "a series of views expressed over an important subject concerning people calling for a solution by influencing the minds of those to whom it is addressed." 'Discourse' is a term used in semantics and discourse analysis, but it also refers to a social concept of discourse. It is often linked with the work of French philosopher, Michael Foucault and Jurgen Habermas's *Theory of Communicative Action* is a seminal volume on this subject. According to him, each thinker, political, social, religious and philosophical, had personal conceptions of 'discourse' which were thought to be incompatible with the other.

The term *discourse* has a broad context in language studies. Discourse analysis is not just one approach, but a series of interdisciplinary approaches that can be used to explore many different social domains in many different types of studies. There is no clear consensus as to what discourses are or how to analyze them. Various scholars and different perspectives offer various definitions of the term discourse and discourse analysis. The preliminary definition of 'discourse' and its relevance to the topic of the thesis is that a discourse is a particular way of talking about and understanding the world or an aspect of the world. Some scholars analyze people's discourse in everyday social interaction, while others prefer a more abstract mapping of the discourses that circulate in society.

In the book *Discourse Analysis:* Theory and Methods by Louise Phillips and Marianne W. Jorgensen, the authors say that discourse is a form of social action that plays a part in producing the social world—including knowledge, identities and social relations—and thereby in maintaining specific social patterns. This view is anti-essentialist: that the social world is constructed socially and discursively implies that its character is not pre-given or determined by external conditions, and that people do not possess a set of fixed and authentic characteristics or essences. Our ways of understanding the world are created and maintained by the social process. Knowledge is created through social interaction in which we construct common truth and compete about what is true and false.

Phillips and Jorgensen's work refers to application of discourse in three different ways. In the most abstract sense, discourse refers to language use as social practice. Discourse is both constitutive and constituted. Discourse is the kind of language used within a specific field such as political or scientific discourse. It also refers to a way of speaking which gives meaning to experience from a particular perspective. The concept refers to any discourse that can be distinguished from other discourses such as a feminist discourse, a neoliberal discourse, a Marxist discourse, a consumer discourse, an environmentalist discourse, a social discourse and such others. Discourse contributes to the construction of social identities, social relations and systems of knowledge and meaning. Thus discourse has three functions, an 'identity' function, a 'relation' function and an 'ideational' function.

In any analysis, two dimensions of discourse are important focal points.

1. Communicative event—an instance of language use such as a newspaper article, a film, a video, an interview or a political speech or a legal argument.

2. The order of discourse—the configuration of all the discourse types which are used within a social institution or a social field. Discourse types consist of discourses and genres.

A 'genre' is a particular usage of language which participates in and constitutes part of particular social practices for example, an interview genre, news or an advertising genre. Examples of orders of discourse include the order of discourse of the media. Within an order of discourse there are specific discursive practices through which text and talk are produced and consumed or interpreted.

In the chapter entitled "The Field of Discourse Analysis" in Louise Phillips and Jorgensen's, *Discourse Analysis:* Theory and Methods the authors discussed at length discourse as a broader social practice. There are, they observed, two aspects to this contextualization. First, the relationship between the discursive practice and its order of discourse is to be explored. It is in the analysis of the relationship between discursive practice and broader social practice, that the questions relating to change and ideological consequences are addressed. The questions that are raised are whether the discursive form reproduces the order of discourse and thus maintains the status quo in the social practice, or whether the order of discourse has been transformed, thereby contributing to social change, as to what the ideological, political and social consequences of the discursive practice are, whether the discursive practice conceals and strengthens unequal power relations in society or whether it challenges power positions by representing reality and social relations in a new way.

Discourse analysis has become one of the most important social constructionist approaches within social psychology. In cognitive approaches to language, written and spoken languages are seen as a reflection of an external world or a product of underlying mental representations of this world. In contrast to cognitivism, discursive psychology treats written and spoken languages as constructions of the world oriented towards social action.

All social constructionist approaches share the structuralist and post structuralist premise. Language, the chief domain of every discourse, is a dynamic form of social practice which shapes the social world including identities, social relations and understandings of the world according to Edward and Potters (1992, 12). This premise entails the view of mental processes and categories as constituted through social, discursive activities rather than as 'internal', as in cognitive psychology and psychoanalysis.

Discourse analysis has become one of the most important social constructionist approaches within social psychology. In cognitive approaches to language, written and spoken languages are seen as a reflection of an external world or a product of underlying mental representations of this world. In contrast to cognitivism, discursive psychology treats written and spoken languages as constructions of the world oriented towards social action.

This book will focus on emancipation of women within these parameters of discourse. Women were shackled in the name of tradition to many undesirable practices of gender discrimination like *sati*, child marriage, restrictions on freedom, and ban on widow marriage that had assumed serious dimensions. It called for a reformative approach which came from reformers like Rammohun Roy for the abolition of *sati*, Jyotirao Phule for rights of women's education, Gandhi for bringing women from private to public domain, and Ambedkar for substantial legal rights for women in Indian society.

Power plays a very important role in discourse. Power has various forms like social structure, law, religion, etc. Emancipation of women questions tradition, especially pertaining to social structures like patriarchy, law, family and religion. This finds illustration in the fact that the reformers opposed the brahmanical system or the system prevailing at that time. Some totally opposed it by questioning the orthodox Hindus, while some wanted to bring a change in the status of women by protecting the tradition and culture which according to them was good for people. They justified the tradition and culture as good, but suggested that tradition was misinterpreted by a chosen few who wanted to dominate and control society. Therefore the discourses of many such reformers were in support of the *Vedas*. But some other reformers who criticized the brahmanical system for being the root of various social evils had to face the wrath of their opponents for challenging the power structure.

This book uses discourse as a form of utterances which plays an important role in producing the social relations and thereby in maintaining specific social patterns. The discourses of the reformers for tackling the problems at their time, the measures taken to ensure the progress of women and the impact of the measures on society in bringing about a change in the attitude of the people are the parameters of analysis here.

While the reformist in Raja Ram Mohan Roy, with a humble beginning, was responsible for the rousing of the consciousness of women from an almost non-existent level, it was Mahatma Jyotirao Phule who brought the awareness and opportunity of education to empower women with knowledge to rise against exploitation, with special reference to women and the lower caste. A traditional and conservative woman of 1920 was brought from home to the public platform under the influence of Mahatma Gandhi, for the freedom movement, which led to the entry of large number of women into the political arena. The long-drawn reform movements over a period of colonial rule took proper shape to recognize a woman's human rights as equal partner in progress, for her liberation by consolidating her rights through legislative means under the leadership of Babasaheb Dr. B.R. Ambedkar at the dawn of Indian independence. These reformers through their works could bring a change in the ideas and actions of their contemporary society which led to women's emancipation countering the power structure of their times.

Consciousness-Raising: Raja Rammohun Roy

Raja Rammohun Roy's voice—both in the oral and written forms—contributed sizably to the issue of women's emancipation. To analyze the distinctive discourse used by him for this purpose, it is essential to first situate his speeches and writings in the specific social context in which they were uttered; in addition, the relationship between the discourse, the speaker/writer and the listener/reader is also significant in order to characterize the basic unit of interaction in terms of parameters such as 'by' and 'for' whom the discourse is produced. (Coulthard 1985, 3) For all this the following discussion serves as a background, before the actual utterances of Rammohun Roy are taken up for analysis.

During the early nineteenth century, India faced numerous social problems of a very serious nature. These problems were not only on account of the British colonial rule in India. They existed earlier too, but the process of colonization seems to have increased our awareness about them. Problems like untouchability, casteism, *sati*, *purdah* and child marriage came to be recognized as serious social evils by the intellectuals during the early 19th century, so they started focusing much of their attention on these problems, which ran parallel to their continued attention towards stepping up the process for the attainment of total political independence.

As a result, the 19th century became a period of social reforms. It is worthy of note that the Indian social reform movement arose from the dominant groups of Indian society such as traders, scribes, renters and tax collectors, who were the backbone of the Indian middle class. Under British colonial rule, this Indian bourgeois society sought to reform itself. The Indian bourgeois initiated campaigns against caste, polytheism, idolatry, child marriage and *sati*. Some reforms were contemplated by the British colonial rulers too, but they could not restructure them in a way that would suit the Indian context. It was at this point of time that Raja Rammohun Roy appeared on the Indian social scene.

Raja Rammohun Roy came from a Radi Kulina Brahman family who descended from Narottama Thakur, a Bengali Vaishnava reformer of the 16th century; this background was one which traditionally enjoyed high social status in the caste hierarchy of Bengal. This sub-caste produced many outstanding personalities including Eshwar Chand Vidya Sagar, Surendranath Banerjee and Ranglal Banarjee. Obviously, when social reformers from this background dominated the social scene, people argued that their social reforms would not only enhance the social and economic position of the emergent middle classes, but also safeguard the interests of the Radi Kulina brahmins. But this was not true, as we see in the case of Rammohun Roy whose major contribution was to bring reforms to the arena of women and their right to life.

Rammohun's father prepared him for government service by arranging for his instructional guidance in Bengali and Arabic. He read the Quran and found monotheism as its base. His mother's family had sent him to Benares where he studied Sanskrit, with special focus on the Vedanta and the Upanishads. His monotheism was reinforced by the teachings of the Vedas.

Back home his rational thinking soon made him oppose the views of the members of his family. His father was extremely orthodox in his approach. It was very difficult to convince him about the new currents of thought which the son subscribed to. So, Rammohun always reacted to the opinions expressed by his father with an elaborate speech beginning with his favorite Bengali word *kintu* meaning 'but'.

Roy's role as a social reformer began in 1804 when he published *Tufat' Ul muwahhidin* (*A Gift to Monotheists*), a tract in

Persian criticizing existing religions as based on irrationality, deception, intolerance and other means of exercising unjust social control.

Roy's zeal for female emancipation was rooted in a series of injustices that were meted out by members of his own family as well as his own experience of living according to unjust social norms. Roy married thrice. He got married when he was a boy. His wife died in childhood. He married for the second time and his second wife bore him two sons. She too died in 1825. His third wife outlived him.

In 1812 an important incident took place in Roy's family which moved him intensely. After the death of his elder brother, Jagamohun in 1812, the widow was forcibly made to die as a *sati*. She was burnt alive on the pyre of her husband. At first she agreed to do it, but later, she requested not to be burnt but her family did not listen to her plea. She was forced to commit *sati*. Her screams shocked Rammohun. Deeply disturbed by her death, he strongly believed that no human being should ever be pressured to kill himself or herself for any reason.

Thereafter, he vigorously preached that *sati* should be abolished. He even visited Calcutta's cremation grounds and pleaded with the widows not to kill themselves in the name of inhuman religious practices. As a part of his crusade against *sati,* he worked towards its abolition through an appropriate order. He wrote an article under the title *A Conference between an Advocate for, and an Opponent of the Practice of Burning Widows Alive* [Part I] published in Bengali and English, in which he based his arguments on Hindu scriptures, tradition and practical morality.

He wrote another article entitled *A Second Conference between an Advocate for, and an Opponent of the Practice of Burning Widows Alive* [Part II], which he dedicated to Lady Hastings on 26 February 1820. In this he based his arguments upon the concept of women's rights.

Roy's contribution to women's emancipation can be seen in his writings on Hindu scriptures in which he offered constructive criticism on the negative aspects of Hinduism. In 1815 Roy formed an association called 'Atmiya Sabha', that is, 'Association of Friends', for the dissemination of religious truth and the promotion of free discussions on theological subjects. The members of the association held theistic worship, studied the Hindu scriptures and organized discussions in which they called for the abolition of practices such as caste system, *sati*, polygamy and dietary restrictions. Roy participated in a debate on idol worship with Subramanya Sastri, a prominent Brahmin of Madras. His success in the debate, however, led a section of people to start a campaign against him and soon he was forced to disband the society.

In 1815, Roy published 'Vedantasara', an essay in Bengali, containing the paraphrase of selected sutras of *Brahmasutra Abhyas*. He also published its English version under the title "Translation of an Abridgement of the Vedanta" the following year. He wrote commentaries in Bengali on Kena, Isa, Katha and Mundaka Upanishads between 1816 and 1819 and published their English versions as well. There was hostile criticism from orthodox Hindu critics against Roy who responded to their publications by writing an article under the title "A Second Defence of the Monotheistical System of the Vedas' ' published in 1820.

Although in his Vedic studies he tried to establish Hinduism as a defensible modern religion in the face of challenges thrown by the Christian religion, his Hindu opponents called him an atheist, a "destroyer of religion" and "a sinful modern". They also objected to his translation of the Upanishads, which they felt most of the people were incapable of understanding. The animosity and enmity of his opponents was so strong that they tried to eliminate him physically through hired killers. He had to face tremendous opposition from the orthodox group of society. The opponents of Roy took adequate counter measures to check his moves.

Radhakanta Dev, as the convenor, established a parallel organization called "Dharma Sabha" to counter the moves of Roy.

One of the positive aspects of colonization was the wider exposure it provided to Indian thinkers and reformers. For instance, Roy's attempt to understand Christianity not only helped him interpret an alien religion but also provided him with a plank to discover the truth that salvation could be attained through service to mankind, which was nothing but akin to the philosophy of 'Advaita' of Hinduism. Roy had first learnt about Christianity around 1816 from Baptist missionaries at Serampore, near Calcutta. The missionaries hoped to attract an influential convert. During 1820 Roy wrote a book about Jesus, emphasizing Christ's moral and ethical sayings. In *The Precepts of Jesus: The Guide to Peace and Happiness,* Roy omitted theological passages and stories about miracles which he thought would discredit Christianity in the eyes of a Hindu and would make Jesus appear to be just another holy man. The book was at once denounced as a perversion of the gospel by Rev. Joshva Mashman, editor of the evangelical publication, *The Friend of India*. Roy was disappointed by this lukewarm response and also because he was labelled a "heathen". He reproved Marshman for un-Christian behavior and defended his distillation of Christianity vigorously in *Appeal to the Christian Public in Defense of the Precepts of Jesus by a Friend of Truth*. He cited the ten commandments of Jesus and the behavioral prescriptions of Mathew and contended that in such passages Jesus had laid out a complete path to salvation through service. Other passages on dogma and history, Roy felt, were rather calculated to do injury by fuelling religious wars and holding Christians up for ridicule. He concluded 'the appeal' with a prayer to God to make religion devoid of differences and discord between man and man, and conducive to the union of mankind.

In his "Second Appeal", 1821, and "Final Appeal", 1823, Roy used a historical/ critical study of Christian scriptures to show that Jesus was not divine and not a part of the Trinity, that salvation came through the teachings of Jesus and not vicarious atonement, and that the holy script had no separate existence.

British and American Unitarians first heard of Roy as a great Hindu monotheist in 1818. The following year his abridgement of the *Vedanta* and *Upanishad* translations and commentaries were reviewed in the British Unitarian monthly repository. He corresponded with Thomas Belsham, Harriet Martineau, Jeremy Bentham and Lant Carpet. News of the precepts controversy and of Roy's conversion of Adam reached America in 1822. Meanwhile, in Calcutta Roy published William Ellery Channing's landmark sermon "Unitarian Christianity", together with a critical review.

In 1822, Roy wrote his tract "Brief remarks regarding modern encroachments on the ancient rights of females according to the Hindu Law of Inheritance". Also, written in 1830, he expounded the law relating to inheritance and alienation of property. So Roy strongly believed in education for Indians, including women. He founded the English language Anglo-Hindu School in 1822 which offered a western style curriculum in English, including science. He opposed the British government sponsored mass education in Sanskrit, claiming that this would marginalize Indians and keep them from joining the modern world. He did, however, also found the Vedanta College in 1826 to educate a few high caste people to read Sanskrit texts. William Adam was disappointed that Roy did not allow the Anglo-Hindu School to be used for Unitarian missionary purposes. Roy, on the other hand, believed that Indians once educated in western culture would develop the theistic ethical values he had long promoted.

'Brahmo Samaj', the brainchild of Rammohun Roy for ushering in social and religious changes within Hindu society, had its initial setbacks. Those who joined it for its ideals left it for its aberrations. Adam reluctantly acquiesced to the creation of the Brahmo Samaj. He reported his analysis of Roy's motives to Joseph Tuckerman, a leading American Unitarian supporter of Unitarian missionary work in India and a longtime correspondent with

Roy. Adam wrote, "Rammohun Roy, I am persuaded, supports this institution, Brahmo Samaj, not because he believes in the divine authority of the *Ved*, but slowly as an instrument for overthrowing idolatry. To be candid, however, I must add that in my mind he employs Unitarian Christianity in the same way as an instrument for spreading pure and just notions of God without believing in the divine authority of the Gospel." (272)

As many as 309 widows were burnt alive on the pyre of their husbands within the jurisdiction of Calcutta in the year 1828, the year in which the Brahma Sabha was established. It was but natural that the misery and degradation of womanhood should have strongly appealed to the sympathetic heart of Roy. His earnest pleadings on their behalf form an important feature of his writings. He personally translated the Vedas into the Bengali language. The women of India have found no greater defender of their rights than the founder of Brahmoism. He defended the legal rights of women, and devoted all the energies of his noble soul to save them from a cruel death.(Sivanath 47)

In 1831 Roy sailed to England to provide the parliament with a native Indian perspective on judicial and revenue systems in India during the debate over the renewal of the East India company charter to oppose the repeal of the *Sati* Act, to lobby for funds for the Mughal emperor who granted Roy the title, 'Raja' and to undertake a crusade to understand the heart of European civilization.

Rammohun Roy's political career in England was fairly successful. He lobbied for equality under the law for Indian and English people independent of religious affiliation. The Indian Jury Act was passed in 1832. He convinced the British parliament to allow imported salt to compete with the salt monopoly in India. His testimony and *Remarks on the Settlement in India by Europeans, 1832*, led to the charter Act of 1833, allowing Europeans to settle without license, in certain areas of India. He was consulted by the lawyers in the *sati* case and in 1832 he was present during the entire three-day hearing before the Privy Council who upheld

Bentinck's law. He declared rejoicingly, that Indians can no longer be guilty of female murder.

Roy not only fought for the emancipation of women through only one angle, that is abolition of Sati, but he also wrote on property rights. While in England Roy became a partisan of the 1832 Reform Bill. After it was passed, he confessed that, had it failed, he would have renounced the country, and writing to the Unitarian Liverpool merchant, William Rathbone, prayed that the mighty people of England might succeed at last in banishing corruption and selfish interests from public proceedings.

Till 1833 Roy continued to do his political, social and religious work. He was physically exhausted and got into financial troubles. His Unitarian friends, including Bristol minister Lant Carpenter, provided support. They arranged for him to stay with his Hindu servants and his adopted son at the home of Carpenter's daughter, Mary. Roy's general condition of health had been poor since 1825.While in Bristol he contracted meningitis. He died in England on September 27, 1833. Thus ended a life completely dedicated to social reform.

Rammohun Roy's role as a social reformer can be mainly seen in his continuous crusade against the obnoxious social practice of *suttee* (British spelling of *sati,* used by Roy and his contemporaries). Instances of burning of women under the pretext of witchcraft abound in the pages of history all over the world in the middle ages but such cold-blooded destruction of young women on the pretext of their husband's death was unheard of anywhere, except in India.

Roy's crusade against *sati* began in 1811 and was reinforced in 1818 when after a serious study of the law he wrote a tract which created a strong commotion among the orthodox sections of Hindu society. Roy was able to move the government to action, particularly when these cases were found to be increasing in number till 1818.

Roy, an erudite scholar, was assertive in his writings and with a strong sense of confidence he opposed this inhuman crime of his time. He felt deeply for the women who were oppressed by such barbaric practices. He wrote tract after tract exposing the evil effects of the practice of sati when the whole country was indifferent and when the orthodox sections of society were distinctly against any interference with the existing practice. In writing out the tracts, he carried out a deep study of the ancient texts, since he realized that the only means of achieving his objective was to convince the orthodox leaders, for it was they who invariably led or coerced the common people to form their views of what was to be done or not to be done. Unfortunately, this was not by the dictates of people's conscience since redemption was denied to them by their conscience keepers, that is, the zamindars.

Roy read the scriptures thoroughly and interpreted them clearly in his translations from Sanskrit to Bengali to make the common man understand that the practice of sati was an extrapolation in the texts by some law-makers at a later date to control women under the pretext of religion. He also translated the same into English so that he could make the British rulers understand and take action against the crime without any fear. Communication leads to knowledge; so, Roy first wanted to make the common man understand the scriptural writings in which there was no mention of such a cruel practice existing anywhere. He was a scholar who knew many languages. This helped him to understand properly the texts of different religions. He then confidently debated with whoever challenged him. This was nothing but the knowledge which leads to change. The change was to make people think about the inhuman acts that take place in the name of religion. The change he visualized would lead to the progress of society. Ultimately, it was some instances of noteworthy social progress which Roy achieved. This was possible because Roy dedicated his whole life in ridding society of the evils of caste system, polygamy, child marriage, child sacrifice, and widow oppression, including the evil practice of *sati*.

In 1830, he wrote a tract, *Abstract of the Arguments Regarding the Burning of Widows Considered as a Religious Rite*, in which he called *sati* "cruel murder, under the cloak of religion". His persuasive influence made the British ruling seem less coercive. Nevertheless, there was much opposition for the new regulation. Roy's opponents formed a pro-*sati* organization, Dharma Sabha, between, 1830-38 and sent representatives to England to argue against *sati*'s criminalization. To counteract this Roy spoke and wrote extensively.

In writing tracts, Roy carried out a deep study of the ancient texts, since he realized that the only means for achieving his objective was to address his arguments to the orthodox leaders, who invariably led or coerced the common people to action and persuaded them about religious sanctions.

One of the major advantages in concretizing the achievements of Roy was the British rule. This came as a help to implement his ideas. And the ideas brought a change into Indian society. During British rule, the prevalence of liberal thought created a group of intellectuals in society like Roy when he expressed his ideas; there were some Indians who were sincerely concerned. But most of them could not come out of their old tradition and some were afraid of being ostracized from their caste. But Roy was ready to challenge people who subscribed to untenable traditional thought because of his understanding of the issues that were prevalent in India. Also with the invention of the printing machine and the Britishers bringing it to India, Roy found it helpful to circulate his papers among the educated class. He brought out his own newspapers in Bengali to convince people about some outdated aspects of the old tradition which would not lead society towards progress.

It needs to be noted to the credit of the British rulers, who were also thinking seriously about the inequality meted out to the Indian women about which they wanted to do something concrete. The then Governor General of India, Lord William Bentinck, thought over this problem very seriously. He initiated the process of working out a plan on how to deal with this problem because he believed that if they did it on religious grounds then they would have to face problems from the orthodox Indians. To help the issue take shape Roy extended his cooperation which Bentinck took immediately. For Roy also William Bentinck was a means to an end—his aim to give women a new lease of life. Therefore he responded to Bentinck's request immediately.

In 1829, Lord William Bentinck, after holding consultations with Roy, declared *sati* illegal. Roy assured him that this would not violate religious liberty because it was an optional rite and not an inviolate part of the Hindu religion. Roy supported the government's decision, and briefed the officials on how to respond to pro-*sati* petitions. He emphasized the need for spontaneous efforts from the grassroot level.

When William Bentinck disclosed his intention of controlling this evil practice by legal enactment, Roy at first felt that in the case of social problems, legal enactment would be very undesirable; but soon he not only gave approval but assured him all help that he was capable of rendering. Roy had his own view on the "means" of abolition of the practice. However, about "abolition itself", his stand was clear, positive and final. He knew that it was always wise to adopt the means which would least disturb the minds of the common people.

It was inevitable that the law abolishing sati would have some negative repercussions. Some correspondence took place between Bentinck and Roy when the former got upset by the commotion created by the orthodox adherence of Radhakant Dev. Roy said the following to Bentinck: "The practice might be suppressed quietly and unobservedly by increasing the difficulties and by indirect agency of the police." (Das Gupta 14)

In an introductory note or 'Advertisement' to the English version of his translation of the tract on sati to make the Britishers understand his stand he wrote: "The little tract, of which the following is a literal translation, originally written in Bangla, has been for several weeks past in extensive circulation in those parts of the country where the practice of widows burning themselves on the pyre of their husbands is most prevalent. An idea that the arguments it contains might tend to alert the notions that some European gentlemen entertain on the subject has induced the writer to lay it before the British public also in its present dress." (122)

Roy's involvement in issues related to the emancipation of women acquires relevance when viewed from the backdrop of colonial India. Therefore, the prevalent attitudes and behavioral patterns of his contemporary age are to be noted with respect to the colonial era in India. While the majority of the emergent middle class were enamored of the traditional ideas and institutions, the more enterprising among them took the initiative to yoke together *brahmanical* ideology and modern western education and thinking. To Roy, such self strengthening attempts to modernize India meant an opportunity for Indians to acquire proper qualifications for various jobs under the British colonial rule and retain their hegemony in the changing socio-economic scenario of Indian society.

For Roy, supported by the friendly British propertied class, the awakening was an elite and exclusive affair. The more sensitive intermediaries, the clerks, professionals and absentee property owners began thinking about their deplorable social situation and backwardness. Living in Calcutta with English men and women, these intermediaries found many of the social customs practiced by the elites as appealing, especially ones like the enslavement of women, etc. The elite began looking for ways and means to redress the situation. However, taking stock of reality and without looking beyond their caste and class interests, these men tried to improve the conditions of women.

During Roy's times the Indian society belonged, for all practical purposes, to the traditionally powerful groups especially since India was under colonial rule. The colonizers had their own take on many of the issues related to Indian social contexts. For instance, the British intellectuals started reading Sanskrit texts and analyzing them. They started thinking of the inhuman practices as a crime and wanted to fight for the cause of Indian women. This was like a boon to Roy who, with the support of English education, developed and propagated rational thinking. Simultaneously, the British who thought of not interfering with Indian religious matters, now started understanding the religious texts and found no rationale for gender discrimination. This helped Roy in his movement. To bring about a change in the society he needed the help of people who would work for progress as reformers and revolutionaries. He was quick to consolidate the help received from the British to achieve this progress in various aspects of Indian social life. He acknowledged this by saying:

> But as we can now fortunately find many European gentlemen capable of investigating legal questions with but little assistance from learned natives, how happy would it be for the Hindu community, both male and female, were they to enjoy the benefits of the opinion of such gentlemen, when disputes arise, particularly on matters of inheritance. (SWRRR 175)

Roy came to know that common people had fear and respect for the British and learned Indians also had respect for the Britishers because of their liberal ideas and their modern developments which circumscribed the Indians as well. The Britishers needed Indians and symbiotically the Indians too needed the British. Also since the Britishers were rulers, the Indians had to obey their orders. So, Roy thought that he could bring a positive social change by making the British understand and participate in the process. He firmly believed that they would definitely help him in bringing about the change. Therefore, Roy associated closely with the British intellectuals and persuaded his contemporary Indians to also place their faith in them. "I only maintain that the Native community place greater confidence in the honest judgment of European gentlemen than in that of their own countrymen." (SWRRR 175)

Records abound of his confidence in and dependence upon the honest judgment of Europeans, For instance, Roy in his letter to Mrs. Woodford, of Brington, discussed the happenings in India. He was satisfied with the Governor-General because his liberal thoughts made the General address the problem of sati seriously and take concrete steps to stop the practice. He was clear that in the name of religion, sati was being imposed on women by the orthodox people with no religious concurrence or rationale. Roy expressed his gratitude towards him in the following words: "You will, I am sure, be highly gratified to learn that the present Governor-General of India has sufficient moral courage to afford them protection against their selfish relations, who cruelly used to take advantage of their tender feelings in the name and under the cloak of religion." (SWRRR 293)

He wrote this in a letter to his close friend, John Digby, who served as collector. Under him Roy worked as the Diwan. Roy learnt English when he was with Digby and in this way he used to share his thoughts with him. He expressed to Digby that the people of India were possibly more superstitious in performing their religious rites and in their domestic concerns, than the rest of the known nations on the earth. So Roy informed Digby that to prove his point he was now translating the religious text into Bengali to expose all the misinterpretations which are included by some selfish leaders/ heads for their personal gain. Roy's strategy was to convince people with the help of their own scriptures and so he wrote to Digby thus, "have also found Hindus in general more superstitious and miserable, both in performance of their religious rites, . . . I, therefore, with a view of making them happy and comfortable, both here and hereafter, not only employed verbal arguments against the absurdities of idolatry practiced by them but also translated their most revered theological work, namely, Vedant, into Bengali and Hindustani" (SWRRR 295)

Roy continued his communication by expressing with pleasure his satisfaction to Digby that he was to a large extent successful in his movement. Because of this, those people who had earlier blamed him were now coming to him to continue their association with him and his work. He confided, "several of my countrymen have risen superior to their prejudices; many are inclined to seek for the truth; and a great number of those who deserted me have now coincided." (SWRRR 295)

Roy further described to Digby his experience with the self-interested leaders who were all the time opposing him and how they were creating problems for him by threatening the people who supported him. He was disturbed by their actions. At this point of time he found great solace that the British supported him in his movement. This feeling also he explained in the letter written to Digby. "I, however, in the beginning of my pursuits met with the greatest opposition from their self-interested leaders, the Brahmins, and also by my nearest relations; I consequently felt extremely melancholy; in that critical situation, the only comfort that I had was the consoling and rational conversation of my European friends, especially those of Scotland and England." (SWRRR 295)

Roy asked his countrymen to educate women. People in his days used to believe that women were 'destined to damnation'. They had neither the right, nor the ability to acquire rational ideas. But Roy felt that 'reason' was indispensable for humanity, and all women, as a part of humanity, are entitled to it. That was why he spoke out, "How do you accuse them of wanting to understand?.." (Chakravarti 275-76) The argument of his pro-sati contemporaries was that women were inferior in terms of understanding and also did not possess virtuous knowledge. These were reasons enough to keep them under control and sati was a means to this end. Roy with his English education acquired liberal ideas and also developed the quality of reasoning; therefore, he questioned the religious heads about the validity of declaring women as inferior: "As to their inferiority in point of understanding, when did you ever afford them a fair opportunity of exhibiting their natural capacity?" (SWRRR 155)

This hard-hitting rhetorical question indicated clearly that the deprivations faced by women could squarely be blamed on the patriarchal power politics. To make women come out of the inferiority of understanding no action was ever taken as no one had thought about it. The leaders of society just escaped blame by invoking the name of religion. Roy thought deeply about it and concluded that the solution was to educate women. It was because they were denied education they were not capable of taking up meaningful roles in society. Roy noted this in the following words which clearly critique the paradoxical situation: "The worst case was that of women who were denied education and were yet subjected to slights for lack of it." (SWRRR 154)

Roy blamed the pro-sati group by saying that it was they who were doing injustice to women by not giving them proper guidance and help for their development. They did not have any right to blame women for not possessing knowledge.

Though he admitted that women may be deficient in knowledge of day-to-day living in the world, he accorded them a special trait which he called "virtuous knowledge", as is evident in the following: "The women clearly possessed virtuous knowledge, for their lives were 'infinitely more self-sacrificing than men'." (Gosh 363) He argued with great conviction that if women are denied education then in spite of virtuous knowledge they would continue to suffer under the cloak of tradition. Though they had the potential to acquire and utilize knowledge, society failed to provide them with opportunities to thus equip themselves. To support this claim, Roy implored his opponents not to label women as inferior to men. He justified his point by giving examples of some of the intelligent women of the Vedic times.

These were women who had the opportunity to get educated. History shows that women of that time debated with men on important topics and often won those debates. So taking their examples Roy said, "There was no dearth of cultural ladies like Maitreyi, Lilavati and wife of Kalidasa." (Chatterji 37) He blamed the progressive deterioration of this high status of women down the pages of history mainly on their lack of education. He said: "But as you keep women generally void of education and acquirements, you cannot, therefore, in justice pronounce on their inferiority." (SWRRR 155)

Comparing his contemporaries who had the privilege of education to the women whom they oppressed, Roy concluded that educating women was the primary requisite for their emancipation. This impelled him to actively engage himself in securing proper education for women, so that they could acquire even the capacity to manage their husband's property after their death, among other things.

Roy further explains that women were considered lesser creatures and their not being trusted to survive their husbands was not due to their nature but due to their inferior upbringing and education. Roy contended that in everyday life, they lived harsher lives and on the whole behaved better than men. Roy reprimanded, "What I (Rammohun Roy) lament is that seeing the women thus dependent and exposed to every misery, you feel for them no compassion that might exempt them from being tied down and burnt to death". (SWRRR 137)

For instance, to persuade others to this point of view, the kind of discourse he often employed was the interrogative mode—which was significant and thought-provoking, as evident in the following: "If then works without desire are acknowledged by you to be superior to works with desire of fruition, why do you persuade widows to perform works for the sake of fruition, and not recommend to them rather to follow asceticism, by which they may acquire eternal beatitude?" (SWRRR 141)

In a similar manner Roy also wanted to convince his own countrymen that they were perpetrating such discriminating and heinous acts against women which were not according religious practice. For this he said that mistakes are committed by all but to know our mistakes and to rectify them is always recommended. This is not the fight between the reformers and anti-reformers but it is a fight between justice and injustice. And when the matters of justice arise, intellectuals do not consider to what religion they belong to or which country they come from. Their fight is only for justice: "The struggles are not merely between the reformers and anti-reformers but between liberty and tyranny throughout the world, between justice and injustice, and between right and wrong." (SWRRR 293)

His purpose of translating the Sanskrit text into Bengali was to make people understand that in the name of religious texts they were imposing rules on women. He adopted the method of dialogic form in his writing because he might have felt it is a more interesting way to make people understand his discourse. Here he adopts the writing style as an Advocate who is justifying the system and the opponent is arguing and clarifying the doubt that what they are quoting was wrong. Roy was the master of many languages and so he interpreted the meaning of the text word by word. In his arguments he argued that no line of any religious texts explains about this crime. But the religious heads argued with him quoting Angira and other saints. But Roy explained then: "All those passages you have quoted are indeed sacred law; and it is clear from those authorities, that if women perform con-cremation or post-cremation, they will enjoy heaven for a considerable time. But attend to what Manu and others say respecting the duty of widows." (SWRRR 124)

Roy had great regard for Manu, the Hindu law giver, and argued that Manu directs after the death of her husband, the widow should pass her whole life as an ascetic. He said that therefore the laws given by Angira and others whom they quoted being contrary to the law of Manu, cannot be accepted because as per Roy the scriptures declared: "Whatever Manu has said is wholesome;" (SWRRR 125) Roy also justified this by an injunction of the Veda which declares: "By living in the practice of regular and occasional duties the mind may be purified. Thereafter by hearing, reflecting, and constantly meditating on the Supreme Being, absorption in Brahma may be attained. Therefore from a desire during life of future fruition, life ought not to be destroyed." (SWRRR 125) He further questions them: "Why do you not also reconcile the rest of the words of Angira, Harita, and others, with those in which Manu prescribes to the widow the practice of living as ascetic was her absolute duty?" (SWRRR 126)

Roy said that it was in every way improper to persuade the widow to self-destruction by citing passages of inadmissible authority. It was also evident from the authorities that the widows should *voluntarily* quit life, ascending the flaming pile of her husband. But, on the contrary, they bind down the widow along with the corpse of her husband, and then heap over her such a quantity of wood that she cannot rise. This was, in fact, deliberate female murder which Roy opposed and said: "Respecting the sinfulness of such an act, that is mere talk: for . . . Therefore the sin is no cause of alarm". (SWRRR130)

Roy further clarified to his opponents who justified that tying/fastening down widows on the pile was not prevalent throughout Hindustan: "It never was the case that the practice of fastening down widows on the pile was prevalent throughout Hindustan: for it is but of late years that this mode has been followed, and that only in Bengal, which is but a small part of Hindustan." (SWRRR 130)

He further clarified if it were universally practiced, the murders would still be criminal. Roy felt that people did not feel for the women burning in the fire because they had been witnessing from youth the voluntary burning of women amongst their elder relatives, their neighbors and the inhabitants of the surrounding villages; and by observing the indifference at the time when the women were writhing under the torture of the flames, habits of insensibility were produced. To stress this fact he gave the example of animal/human sacrifice in certain religious sects as opposed to others who abhor such practices: "like the worshippers of female deities who, witnessing from their infancy the slaughter of kids and buffaloes, feel no compassion for them in the time of their suffering death, while followers of Vishnu are touched with strong feelings of pity." (SWRRR 131)

He was annoyed at the explanation of his opponents that the family of women forced to commit sati would be free from apprehensions and also the husband be assured that his wife would not go astray. To counter this argument, Roy questioned, "But is there not also a danger of a woman going astray during the life-time of her husband." (SWRRR,131) Roy reiterated that even *Smarta Bhattacharya, Sastras, Vasishtha* never spoke of sati by force but left the choice to individual women. Roy quoted from the Veda: "Knowledge and rites both offer themselves to man; but he who is possessed of wisdom, taking their respective nature into serious consideration, distinguishes one from the other, and chooses faith, despising fruition; while a fool, for the sake of advantage and enjoyment, accepts the offer of rites". (SWRRR 135)

This passage is a significant example of Roy's unique discourse, especially explicating his chosen ideology. It illustrates, as Norman Fairclough in *Analyzing Discourse* suggests, "the effects of [a] text(s) inculcating ideologies. As Fairclough declares: "Ideologies are representations of aspects of the world which can be shown to contribute to establishing, maintaining and changing social relations of power, domination and exploitation." (idbi)

By applying these parameters to the words of Roy, we can clearly explicate how he is changing existing ideologies as well as inculcating new ones. He is questioning the power structures prevalent in the society of his times in order to bring about change/reform. In the above passage as well as in many others quoted in the present book, Roy has outlined the ideology of domination and exploitation—in fact, his entire effort of women's emancipation can be seen as a discourse addressed to reformulating social relations, especially those pertaining to gender. Continuing in a similar vein, Roy argued: "For we find in the text of *Harita* and *Vishnu*, the phrase *Pravivesahutasanam,* which means ``entering the flames", and the term *Samaroh Dharisanam*, signifying 'ascending the flames'. You have interpreted these directions in this way; that, a considerable distance from the pile, fire may be placed and a piece of grass or rope. . . . You must then, before you can justify your murder of helpless women, prepare a new dictionary; but there is no great probability of its interpretations being adopted by men of knowledge." (SWRRR 151)

Roy explained that performing sati with the consent of the widow was not a crime. He quoted some incidents to prove it. According to the Sastras, numberless women, in all ages, who were desirous of final beatitude, living as ascetics, attained their object. Evidence of this is to be found in the *Mahabharata* and other works: "The widows of the heroic Kurus, who fell valiantly with their faces to the foe, and were translated to the heaven of Brahma, performed only the prescribed ceremonies with water and did not burn themselves on the piles of their husbands. I have; moreover, to request your attention to the fact that in the three instances you have quoted the very words "entered into fire" are used." (SWRRR 153)

By stressing on the voluntary nature of self-immolation as acceptable, Roy is inculcating a sense of autonomy in women, something that the social power structures have been denying to them. Addressing his male audience, he insists that enforced self-sacrifice is no better than willful murder:

> In these three cases, then, it appears that the widows actually entered the flames, and therefore whatever widow in the present time does not enter the flames, but is burnt to death by others tying her down to the pile, has not performed the ceremony according to the ancient

> practice you have instanced; and from rites so performed she cannot even be entitled to the temporary enjoyment of heavenly pleasures; and those who tie her down, and pressing on her with bamboos, kill her, must, according to all Sastras, be considered guilty of the heinous crime of woman-murder. (SWRRR 153-54)

When the opponents were questioned why they tie the widow with rope with the dead body before burning her, the opponents said that women by nature are inferior in understanding, without resolution, unworthy of trust, subject to passion, and void of virtuous knowledge. Roy believed and he also proved that women were superior to men and said: "By ascribing to them all sorts of improper conduct, you have indeed successfully persuaded the Hindu community to look down upon them as contemptible and mischievous creatures, whence they have been subjected to constant miseries." (SWRRR 54) This passage is significant not only as an example of Roy's commitment to women's emancipation by establishing their self-worth, but also from the point of view of discourse analysis. As Linda A Wood and Relf O Krogen (2000) have pointed out, there is "potential importance of absence, 'What is not there,' in both discourse excerpts and the discourse as a concentrate not only on what the speaker is saying but also on what he is doing, not only on what is said but also on what is left out. (ibid)

Analyzed from this perspective, the above words of Roy acquire multi-faceted significance. On the surface he is chiding the leaders of society for their discriminative attitude towards women. The words have deeper connotation to the changes Roy expects in the male attitude towards women. Without making it obvious verbally, he is implying that for women's emancipation the primary requirement is to accord them respect. Unless society looks upon them as worthy, they will continue to be oppressed, ill-treated and murdered.

As a reformer with a positive and balanced perspective, Roy used irrefutable logic to put forth his view of women's worth. He said: "Women are in general inferior to men in bodily strength and energy; consequently the male parts of the community, taking advantage of their corporal weakness, have denied to them those excellent merits that they are entitled to by nature." (SWRRR 154)

Such words, spoken as they were to his male contemporaries, aimed at bringing about a new awareness about gender relationships, have a consciousness-altering impact on women too. They began to alter their own perspective about their inherent potential and its concretization. Roy declared that their mental strength was more than men: "You charge them with want of resolution . . . in a country where the name of death makes the male shudder, that the female, from her firmness of mind, offers to burn with the corpse of her deceased husband; and yet you accuse those women of deficiency in point of resolution" (SWRRR 155)

To strengthen his argument of women's excellence Roy proferred many arguments and he continues: "With respect to their subjection to the passions, this may be judged of by the custom of marriage as to the respective sexes; for one man may marry two or three, sometimes even ten wives and upwards; while a woman, who marries but one husband, desires at his death to follow him, forsaking all worldly enjoyments, or to remain leading the austere life of an ascetic." (SWRRR 155-56)

He further says that we should not omit the present opportunity of offering up thanks to Heaven, whose protecting arms have rescued our women from cruel murder, under the cloak of religion, and our character, as a people, from the contempt and pity with which it has been regarded, on account of this custom by all civilized nations on the surface of the globe. Since the practice was more prevalent in Bengal, Roy addressed many to his remarks of that state and through comparison, indicated his point of view thus: "It cannot pass unnoticed by those who are acquainted with the state of society in India, that the number of female suicides in the single province, is almost ten to one: we may safely attribute this disproportion chiefly to the greater frequency of a plurality of wives among the natives of Bengal, and to their total neglect in providing for the maintenance of their females." (SWRRR 156)

These hard-hitting arguments convinced many to change their attitudes and actions. In spite of his powerful persuasive discourse, some dissidents still remained. These conservative elements led by Raja Ramakant Deb (1784-1867) refuted the texts cited by Roy and his fellow reformers to prove, with authentic instances, that *sati* had the sanction of the *shastras.* The reactionaries and the reformers both swore by the same sacerdotal texts as their authority. Both sides delved into the *shastras* to prove their point and build their cases on the past precedents to resolve current controversies.

Roy taking passages from the same religious text which were followed by the pro-sati leaders brought out the misinterpretations of the text by them. Then he questioned, "And do you consider how great is the sin to kill a woman; therein forsaking the fear of God, the fear of conscience, and the fear of the *Sastras,* yet from a dread of the reproach of those who delight in female murder?" (SWRRR 130)

Roy argued that to keep somebody in control they should not take law in their hand and dictate terms only because they have power in their hands. Everyone has to fear God and interact accordingly with others. They have to show the right path to others but not by punishing them. He angrily explains, "Control alone cannot restrain from evil thoughts, words, and actions; but the suggestions of wisdom and fear of God may cause both man and woman to abstain from sin. Both the *Sastras* and experience show this." (SWRRR 131)

Roy delved into the reason for sati by pointing to the economic and power structures of society. In addition, there was also the question of family pride. The religious heads feared that after the death of the husband, if his wife chooses another man, it would be a disgrace not only to the family of that particular woman but to the society as a whole. To protect women from this type of crime, the custom was adopted, they declared. Also, we find that some kings felt complacent that their wife or wives would follow them even in their death. On this point Roy argues that if a wife dies immediately her husband marries another. Even in her lifetime he marries more than once. Here he points out to a glaring instance of gender discrimination. Discourse is often a determiner of ideology. Roy takes an ideological stance here to hint at the gender equality which was missing in the society of his times. Women were never allowed polygamy and even after the death of the husband she was not allowed to marry again. She would happily forsake all wordy enjoyments and remain ascetics for life or follow him even in his death. To emphasize this he cited that in the Vedic period the inhuman custom of self-immolation of the widow was forbidden among the progressive individuals and groups of the population.

When Roy published *Tufat' Ul muwahhidin* (A Gift to Monotheists), a tract in Persian he was criticizing some aspects of certain existing religions as based on irrationality, deception, intolerance and other means of unjust social control. He advocated, instead, faith in "one being" and the universal morality of doing no harm to others. He further affirmed, "Every person should exercise his own intellectual power with the help of acquired knowledge to discern good from bad, so that his valuable divine gift should not be left useless." (Chatterji 206).

This is the equation Roy used for his reform movement. He considered intellect alone insufficient. Supported by knowledge, intellect would become a divine gift which he used for progressive social reform like the setting up of Brohmo Samaj. 'Brahmo Samaj', was formed for ushering in social and religious changes within the Hindu society in which women were given a central role and responsibilities. Therefore, his ideals as enshrined in the canon of Brahmo Samaj exemplify his crusade for women's emancipation.

Roy's perception about the problems relating to women led him to work towards changing the Indian society from being orthodox to being modern. The tiny middle-class intelligentsia that Rammohun Roy led was culturally rooted in a Sanskrit background. Since they could not transgress their *shastric* traditions they showed amazing intelligence in combining modern ideas with those of conservative *Brahminical* ideology.

Mentioned above is an excellent example of this form, among his writings, called "*Conference between an Advocate for and an Opponent of the practice of burning widows alive*". This is a dialogue arguing for and against sati, the practice of encouraging—and often forcing—windows to burn themselves alive on their husband's funeral pyres, here referred to as "Concremation." As has been mentioned, this practice was outlawed by the British mainly due to the efforts of Roy. Consequent to his vision, today sati is rare, as are the polygamous arrangements which he describes; but many of his comments on the burdens borne by women are applicable even now.

The impact of such a discourse on the recipient is bound to be powerful. Many people were deeply influenced by Roy's opinions and a new level of social awareness arose among the intelligentsia. Roy not only showed them their mistake but also said any religion on this earth will not teach people to commit a crime. His contention was that when society was at fault, it needed to be pointed out. But often people become angry when this is done, while others accept it and correct their mistakes. He hoped that his argument would have a beneficial and transformative effect to end the negatives in society especially pertaining to women.

To garner support for the women's cause, Roy used that variety of discourse which would win compassion for women. He constantly emphasized the disadvantaged position of women in order to halt their further degradation. Women, according to him deserved a better deal, instead of twisting the *shastric injunctions* to torture them.

All these helped strengthen Roy's reformative zeal and he established himself as a foremost voice of social change. Modern

Hindu social reformers cannot be expected to possess his faith in the sacred books where two courses were prescribed for the widow: one as 'ascetic life' or '*anumarana*' or postcremation. But the earlier codes prescribed quite a different course that is *niyoga,* an appointment analogous to the Jewish Levirate, a custom by which a dead man's brother or next of kin or even a member of the same caste could marry the widow. The widow was first made to lie down by her dead husband on the funeral pyre. She was then aided to rise and return home with the recitation of the following stanza which occurs both in the Rigveda (X188) and the Atharva Veda (XVIII-3.1): "Go up, o' woman to the world of living; thou liest by this one who is deceased; come to him who grasps thy hand, thy second spouse thou hast now entered into the relation of wife to husband." (Das Gupta 24)

Roy very affectively, and with authority said that if the practice of female murder continues like this then we cannot think of progress which is the stepping stone for improvement. So Roy comes out saying that it is every Indian's duty to make ignorant people come out of this superstitious belief, understand the fact and act to improve the condition of women in society.

According to Roy the major hurdle in the path of women's emancipation was because of polygamy among Brahmans which was directly contrary to the law given by ancient authors. Yajnavalkya, authorized second marriages, while the first wife is alive only under eight circumstances.

Roy had fired his first salvo on polygamy in Atmiya Sabha in condemnation of not only the inhuman practice of *sati* but also other social evils. In the tract, *Brief remarks regarding modern encroachments on the ancient rights of females according to the Hindu Law of inheritance*, Roy said, "It had become almost a practice for Brahmins to take two, three, four or even more wives of tender age for a trivial consideration or for other reasons." (170)

The dire consequences arising from polygamy were obvious from the fact that the widows after the death of their husbands lived a miserable life as slaves without having any hope of support, struggle to make a living or die on the funeral pyre of their husbands for applause and honour from those assembled around the pyre.

Another kind of suffering was the role of the widow as either mother or stepmother. The consequences could be that the woman who was the sole mistress of the family the day before, on the next day became dependent on her sons and subject to the slights of her daughters-in-law. The cruel sons often would wound the feelings of the dependent mother, deciding in favour of their own wives, when disputes took place between their mothers and wives. Because of polygamy, the stepmothers suffered intensely.

To escape this fate worse than death, women often chose sati. So the only way to remove this evil was to improve the lot of women, especially widows, Roy believed. If society accused widows of misdemeanor, this also he attributed to their helplessness and misery. He exhorted society again and again to increase women's capabilities to take care of themselves, independently. As he said: "In general, however, a consideration of the difficulties attending a lawsuit, which a native woman, particularly a widow, is hardly capable of surmounting, induces her to forego her right; and if she continues virtuous, she is obliged to live in a miserable state of dependence, destitute of all the comforts of life; it too often happens, however, that she is driven by constant unhappiness to seek refuge in vice." (SWRRR 175)

Through his writings, speeches and debates Roy proved that in the name of religion even the good people were committing a crime. He warned them that if they did not understand the wrongs done in the society then they would lead the nation on the wrong path. For this, reasoning is very important. Roy advised people to think over any issue and analyze it before blindly following anything. Just because something is written in a religious text or spoken by someone who has not properly understood and might not have interpreted it properly, we follow the wrong path. All this is the effect of misdirected power in society. Roy warns people against this and hopes for some correctives; "Experience shows that unchecked power often leads the best men wrong, and produces general mischief." (SWRRR 175) in contrast, he upholds laudable qualities in women. Roy gives examples about the trustworthiness of women. Women are blamed for not being trustworthy. Roy suggests they look into the cases of men deceiving women which are many more than women deceiving men. "With regard to trustworthiness . . . I presume that the number of the deceived women would be ten times greater than that of the betrayed men." (SWRRR 155)

Traditional marriage, according to Roy, had its own disadvantages as far as women were concerned. In this too he reiterates the point that women have inherent greatness: "As long as the husband is poor, she suffers every kind of trouble, and when he becomes rich, she is altogether heart-broken. All this pain and affliction their virtue alone enables them to support." (SWRRR 156)

Roy unveils numerous sufferings of a woman: the injustice done to her, the control over her by society, imposing restrictions on her in the name of religion etc. Roy's deep concern made him discuss point by point the various reasons why she was kept away from all her rights. For instance, a girl is the same child who shares her happiness with her brother in the house of their father. But she has no right over the property along with her brother. He empathizes with women who are thus deprived by saying: "How distressing it must be to the female community and to those who interest themselves in their behalf, to observe daily that several daughters in a rich family can prefer no claim to any portion of the property, whether real or personal, left by their deceased father, if a single brother be alive: while they (if belonging to a kulin family or Brahman of higher rank) are exposed to be given in marriage to individuals who have already several wives and have no means of maintaining them" (SWRRR 174)

He very clearly takes each and every point to prove that in the name of religion, selfish men have made these rules. And women of this society at that time had no say in formulating them. First of all women were not given any opportunity to think over her problems. They were just made to think that it was their duty to suffer. If they did not do so, the whole family would be affected. They were kept in the clutches of superstition. Women had no voice in society. Therefore they needed the voice of men like Roy to speak for them. Roy took this responsibility seriously and enumerated many evils perpetrated against women.

The kind of discourse Roy used to support the cause of women was thus determined by the social, religious and political contexts of his contemporary times. His words were not addressed to women. Rather he was speaking/ writing for men. He was doing this on behalf of women but not as their voice. His discourse clearly illustrates a male voice talking to men on the topic of women's emancipation based on the exposure he had to global thought currents due to the British rule in India. He was also fulfilling the social requirement that became foregrounded in the rapidly changing scenario of 19th century India. These become evident as we read some of his words in different contexts—all of them concentrating on women's emancipation. Here one needs to keep in mind that discourse is not merely the structures of the English language he is using, but the wider frames of experience which he projects through the medium of the English language. His distinctive discourse depends much on the kind of English he uses, the fluency with which he uses it and the impact it has on the listener/reader as well as the change it has engendered in society.

Emancipation through Education: Mahatma Jyotirao Phule

To analyze the concept of discourse a significant point is to determine the various functions a piece of writing, an utterance or an idea performs. (Coulthard 3). When applied to the male voices crusading for women's emancipation in colonial India, this aspect of discourse analysis needs to be kept in mind. For instance, Jyotirao Phule's emphasis on women's education as incipient as well as extraneous functions not only for bringing about social reform but also for the evolution of social consciousness through increased awareness of the sad plight of women and the need for their upliftment. All these become evident from the following discussions as well as writings of Phule.

As was evident in the chapter on Raja Rammohun Roy during the nineteenth century, the Reforms Movement paved a way to a series of social changes in Indian society. The contributions made by different reformers instilled a sense of confidence in the minds of people and prepared them to take part in India's struggle for freedom against British colonial rule. The relentless fight waged by the reformers shook the foundation of British colonial rule in India. For the emancipation of women, Raja Rammohun Roy fought against the criminal social evil of sati, while Jyotirao Phule fought against the inhuman treatment of orthodox Brahmins towards Shudras, Atishudras and women. His role as a social reformer marks the beginning of social discourse of equality for all through education.

Jyotirao Phule occupies a unique position among the social reformers of Maharashtra in the nineteenth century. He revolted against the unjust caste system under which millions of people had suffered for centuries. In particular, he courageously upheld the cause of the untouchables and took up cudgels for the poorer peasants. He was a militant advocate of their rights. The story of his stormy life is an inspiring saga of a continuous struggle which he waged relentlessly against the forces of reaction. Though some keen observers of the social scene in Maharashtra like Narayan Mahadeo Parmananda did acknowledge his greatness in his lifetime, it is only in recent decades that there is increasing appreciation of his service and sacrifice in uplifting the masses.

Before we look into the ideas of Jyotirao Phule and his contribution towards female emancipation in colonial India, it is necessary to know his profile, his birth and parentage. Jyotirao was born in 1827 to Govindrao and Chimnabai. His father, Govindrao was a vegetable-vendor at Poona. Originally Jyotirao's family known as Gorhays, came from Katgun, a village in the Satara district of Maharashtra, His grandfather Shetiba Gorhay settled down in Poona. Since Jyotirao's father and two uncles served as florists under the last of the Peshwas, they came to be known as `Phule'. Jyotirao's mother passed away when he was hardly one year old. After completing his primary education, Jyotirao Phule had to leave school and help his father by working on the family farm. Phule's marriage was celebrated when he was not even thirteen.

The presence of the British in India brought about profound changes in the social and administrative conditions of the country, and these, in turn, affected the educational policy of the Government. The impulse towards reform came from two sources: the need for public servants with knowledge of English and the influence in favour of both English and vernacular education which was exercised by the missionaries in the early years of the nineteenth century. During this transition period, when the doors of education were ajar for low-caste students, some wise and far-seeing men sent their children to school. Govindrao too, thought it wise to send his son to school. At the age of seven, Phule began his rudimentary studies at a Marathi school. As a boy, he faced many obstacles in getting school education. As his father was misled by an orthodox Brahmin, Phule was withdrawn from the school. But his intellect and energy attracted the attention of some well-intentioned neighbours. Among such neighbours were two learned men. They both impressed upon Govindrao the necessity of education to his son and urged him to give a chance for the betterment of his mind and future. Thus Phule got the opportunity to go to a missionary school at Poona.

It was in this school that he met Sadashiv Ballal Govande, a Brahmin, who remained a close friend throughout his life. Both Phule and Govande were greatly influenced by Thomas Paine's ideas and they read Paine's famous book *The Rights of Man* with great interest. Moro Vithal Valvekar and Sakharam Yashwant Paranjapye were two other Brahmin friends of Phule who in later years stood by him in all his activities. After completing his secondary education in 1847, Phule decided not to accept a job under the Government. The inspiration he had derived from the American freedom struggle was deep-rooted, profound and pulsating in his view. He was engrossed in the thoughts of the equality of man, the rights of man and the freedom of man. Phule said to himself that he was well-educated. He knew what was good and what was evil. He belonged to the religion to which Brahmins belonged. Then his question was what led them to believe that he was inferior to them. He questioned whether it was religion that made them behave like that. But religion was the relation between man and God. He then came to the conclusion that the Brahmins enjoyed power as a priestly class and as the head of the caste system. So he realized that caste was the cause of all problems, the enemy of solidarity, of organized and cultural life. Brahmanism was the outer form of its expression. In order to annihilate Brahmanism that condemned the non-Brahmins to perpetual subordination and humiliation, he concluded that the idea that *heredity is the basis of society* must be discarded. Phule's participation in the marriage procession of a Brahmin bridegroom who as his friend invited a great deal of wrath from orthodox Brahmin elders. These two incidents brought about a great deal of change in his outlook.

The caste system was solid, unbreakable and enduring. Because the lower classes had no education, they had accepted this mental slavery. Phule thought to open the gates of knowledge to the lower classes by disseminating education among them. He identified that India had kept women and the shudras out of the pale of education. He had realized the truth of the proverb, 'the hand that rocks the cradle rules the world.' So he decided to open a school for girls, as he thought that women were the guides of the destinies of their children and if they knew their duty well, the nation would improve considerably.

Phule rose in revolt against inequality. He worked for female emancipation creating an awakening among them through education. He threw a challenge to the orthodox Hinduism. He challenged traditions and the Manusmriti. He vehemently condemned Manu's injunctions. The tradition-mongers shouted: "Orthodox is our doxy! Our religion is in danger. Jyotirao is an enemy of society. He is a nobody and a descendant of a generation of nobodys!" (Keer 25)

The Poona Brahmins hotly debated this unfamiliar attack on their religion and they regarded Phule's work as a disgrace to the holy city. Their hatred for Phule knew no bounds. They said had Phule performed such a vile deed at the time of the Peshwa rule, he would have been trampled under the elephant's feet. But they were powerless now. They threatened Phule through men of his own caste with serious consequences. But their threats were of no avail.

Phule could not get the services of a teacher to help him in the school he had started, so he took the help of his wife, Savitribai, whom he had taught at home. A wave of uncontrollable excitement and anger swept across Poona. The learned Brahmins and their hirelings hated the very sight of Savitribai. In India women teachers had practically disappeared from the scene by the beginning of the Christian era. It was after Savitribai Phule had appeared on the scene that Indian women began to take part in public work. Great social changes do not occur accidentally. They are willed by men of action. Today Savitribai is called as the first woman teacher of modern India.

In 1868, Phule decided to give untouchables access to a small bathing tank in his house. In his controversial book called *Slavery* published in June 1873, Phule included a manifesto which declared that he was willing to dine with all regardless of their caste, creed or country of origin. It is significant that several newspapers refused to give publicity to the manifesto because of its contents.

However the orthodox Brahmins of Poona exerted their social pressure on Phule's father, Govindarao. Phule's father yielded to their wicked pressure. Govindrao asked his son more in sorrow than in anger to leave either the school or the house. With a sad heart, Phule told his genial father frankly, "Even at the risk of life I shall not give up the cause." (Keer 27) Phule's father asked his son and the daughter in-law to leave his house as both of them refused to give up their noble endeavor.

Phule's contribution towards female emancipation through education continued in spite of several obstructions. On September 17, 1851 Phule started another girls' school at *Rasta Peth* and the third school on March 15, 1852 at *Vetal Peth.* Dadoba Panduranga Tarkhedar, Superintendent of Government Vernacular schools inspected the school at Budhwar Peth on October 16, 1851, and expressed satisfaction at the progress of the girls. He said that it was creditable, considering the short time the school had conducted its work. The course of tuition comprised reading of the *Neethi Bodh Katha* and writing in *Bal Bodh* characters, distinguishing parts of speech, explaining geographical terms, doing subtraction, learning the history of the Marathas and reading the maps of Asia, Europe and India.

On February 17, 1852, Phule's school was publicly examined. A vast crowd of citizens assembled to witness the function. After the examination was over, Justice Bhan Sahab Manday said in a speech that he was sorry that the citizens assembled there had not so far realized the importance of female education. Quoting the great English epic poet Milton, Brown, the Judge, said that happiness and usefulness would bless the home if women were educated. He was glad at least some natives were thinking in the right direction and trying to uplift the country.

Colonial India was one in which persons like Phule had felt some sense of security. The laws of the colonizer were such that the shudras, ati shudras and women were protected from the excesses of orthodox Brahmins. But Phule was not a supporter of colonization. He was firm in his conviction that the British came to India because the Hindus were divided by caste system. He thought that there was disunity and lack of real patriotism. Therefore the British had succeeded in imposing their rule on India. He was not sympathetic, but apathetic towards the revolutionary struggle that was raging all over India to overthrow the colonial power. Yet because of his patriotic antecedents and independent spirit of mind, he was shunned during the days of this rebellion by European friends and admirers. They had watched his activities with no little suspicion. Since then Phule resolved not to visit Europeans except on invitation. Later he never sought interviews with them. An incident which revealed his attachment for the poor peasant shows his courage in drawing the attention of a member of the British royal family to the sufferings of the farmers in rural areas. On 2 March 1888, Hari Raoji Chiplunkar, a friend of Phule, arranged a function in honor of the Duke and Duchess of Connaught. Dressed like a peasant, Phule attended the function and made a speech. He commented on the rich invitees who displayed their wealth by wearing diamond studded jewellery and warned the visiting dignitaries that the people who had gathered there did not represent India. Phule suggested that they ought to visit some nearby village as well as the areas in the city occupied by the untouchables. Phule requested the Duke of Connaught who was a grandson of Queen Victoria to convey his message to the queen and made a strong plea to provide education to the poor people, Phule's speech created a great stir.

Phule opened two more girl's schools during 1851-52 in a memorial addressed to the Education Commission (popularly known as the Hunter Commission) in 1882; in this he described his activities in the field of education. On 11 May 1888, a big public meeting was organized in Pune in recognition of the impact of his theoretical—instructional and agitational—organizational work and fondly conferred on him the title *Mahatma.*

Phule was aware that primary education among the masses in the Bombay Presidency was very much neglected. According to him the policy of the British Government resulted in the virtual monopoly of all the higher offices under the Government by the Brahmins. Phule boldly attacked the stranglehold of the Brahmins, who prevented others from having access to all the avenues of knowledge and influence. He denounced them as cheats and hypocrites. He asked the masses to resist the tyranny of the Brahmins. All his writings were variations on this theme. His critics made fun of his ignorance of grammar and philology, his inelegant language and far-fetched interpretation of Indian history and the ancient texts. They brushed his criticism aside by saying that he was merely echoing what the Christian missionaries had said about Indian society in general and Brahmins in particular. The established scholars of his time did not take Phule's arguments seriously. His critics did not realize that Phule's acrimonious criticism was basically a spontaneous outburst of genuine concern for the equal rights of human beings Emotionally he was so deeply involved in his work that he could not make a dispassionate analysis and take a detached view of the social forces. Jyotirao's deep sense of commitment to basic human values made it difficult for him to restrain himself when he witnessed injustice and atrocities committed in the name of religion by those who were supposed to be its custodians.

Widow remarriages were banned and child-marriage was very common among the Brahmin and other upper castes in the then Hindu society. Many widows were young and not all of them could live in a manner in which the orthodox people expected them to live. Some of the delinquent widows resorted to abortion or left their illegitimate children to their fate by leaving them on the streets. Out of pity for the orphans, Phule established an orphanage, possibly the first such institution founded by a Hindu. He gave protection to pregnant widows and assured them that the orphanage would take care of their children. It was in this orphanage run by Phule that a Brahmin widow gave birth to a boy in 1873 and Phule adopted him as his son.

For some time, Phule worked as a contractor for the government and supplied building material required for the construction of a huge barrage at Khadakwasla near Pune. He had the direct experience of working with the officials of the Public Works Department which was notorious as a hotbed of corruption. Except the British officers holding very high positions in the Department, the clerks and other officers were invariably Brahmin and they exploited the illiterate workers. Phule felt it necessary to explain to the workers how they were duped by the Brahmin officials. In one of the ballads composed by him, he described vividly the fraudulent practices resorted to by the Brahmin officials in the Public Works Department.

In 1855, he wrote a play *Tritya Ratna* exposing the claims and beliefs expressed in the Puranas in the name of God. There is a strong polemic against idol-worship through which he gives the message that knowledge is better than worship of idols.

Phule did perform the obsequies of his father, but not as ordained in the Brahmin *Shastras*. In accordance with his rational views of life, he performed them. He did not believe in offering lumps of flour to crows as an obligation to the deceased and his ancestors! Instead he gave a dinner for the poor and the crippled and distributed books and other articles to students. He did the same thing even on the death anniversary of his father.

Phule vehemently opposed the evil practice of Sati. Although the problem of remarriage of widows was confined to Brahmins and some other high caste Hindus, Phule was moved by the miserable condition of the widows and often by their immoral behavior. Sometimes they were involved in child murder. Being a man of flaming indignation against injustice, Phule actively supported the movement for widow remarriage. He wanted to liberate women from their age-old shackles. It is said that Phule encouraged the marriage of a Shenavi widow in 1864. Great reforms are the result of a series of small pioneering efforts.

In 1876, Phule was nominated as a member of the Poona Municipality. He tried to help people in the famine-stricken areas of Maharashtra when a severe famine in 1877 forced people in the rural area to leave their villages. Some of them had to leave their children behind and an appeal issued on 17 May 1877 by Phule indicates that the Victoria Orphanage was founded under the auspices of the *Satya Shodhak Samaj* to look after these unfortunate children. From the beginning of the year 1879, Krishnarao Bhalekar, one of his colleagues, edited a weekly called *Deenbandhu* which was the organ of the Satya Shodhak Samaj. The weekly wrote about the grievances of the peasants and workers.

In his booklet called *Satsara* (The Essence of Truth) published in June 1885, he criticized the Brahmo Samaj and the Prarthana Samaj. On 24 September 1873, Jyotirao convened a meeting of his followers and admirers and it was decided to form the *Satya Shodhak Samaj* (Society of Seekers of Truth) with Phule as its first president and treasurer. The main objectives of the organization were to liberate the Shudras and ati shudras and to prevent their exploitation by the Brahmins. All the members of the *Satya Shodhak Samaj* were expected to treat all human beings as children of God and worship the Creator without the help of any mediator. Membership was open to all and the available evidence proves that some Jews were also admitted as members.

Phule refused to regard the Vedas as sacrosanct. He opposed idolatry and denounced the chaturvarna. In his book *Sarvajanik Satya Dharma Pustak* published in 1891, his views on religious and social issues are given in the form of a dialogue. According to him, both men and women were entitled to enjoy equal rights and it was a sin to discriminate among human beings on the basis of sex. He stressed the unity of man and envisaged a society based on liberty, equality and fraternity. He was aware that religious bigotry and aggressive nationalism destroy the unity of man.

Throughout his life Jyotirao Phule fought for the emancipation of the downtrodden people and the struggle which he launched at a young age ended only when he died on 28 November 1890. He was a pioneer in many fields and among his contemporaries he stands out as one who never wavered in his quest for trust and for justice. His goal of action was 'rights of man' without any difference between Brahmins and non-Brahmins, between men and women.

Jyotirao Phule's contribution to female emancipation was significant. During his own lifetime, he spoke and wrote about rights, liberties, and democracy of the downtrodden. His Abhangs, Akhandas, Ballads, Opinions, Letters, Conversations, Street Plays, Advices, Warnings, Memorials and Memoranda of Appeals to the British, contain his ideas and ideals. They were on the cruel, tyrannical and unequal laws imposed by Brahmins, setting up of foundling homes, and on foundling home systems.

Phule appealed for female education. The appeal for female and low caste education given by Phule strongly reflects his opinion about education of women in India and its place among the civilized nations of the earth as a society to improve materially and intellectually. According to misquoted religious scriptures, women had no right to education. If educated, a woman would abandon home and destroy happiness. This was propagated as the contention of the *Shastras*. Women's education meant a sacrilegious act against caste and society to the orthodox Brahmins. Phule endeavoured to remove the hegemonic structure of knowledge by Brahmins. This was a momentous achievement in view of the fact that he was the first low caste person to forcefully make his voice heard and heeded.

Jyotirao Phule was particularly receptive to the religious and social traditions that ordained a woman to live in dependency to the man. He held the view that education gives women and Shudras independence from people in power and imparts happiness.

But the education should be through non-Brahmins. In his book *Cultivators Whipcord*, he muses,

> For want of education intellect deteriorated
> For want of intellect morality decayed
> For want of progress wealth vanished
> For want of wealth Shudras perished
> All these sorrows sprang from illiteracy. (Keer 182)

Significantly Phule's writings integrated caste, gender, equality and liberation of the downtrodden through education. Phule's belief in the power of education was to liberate the marginalized and provide new modes of social perception to them which culminated in reforms for women.

Through his writings Jyotirao Phule threw a challenge to Manusmriti and declared to the people deprived of education that it was only education which will give them happiness,

> Follow me, falter not now, Down with Manu's injunctions
> Education imparts you happiness
> Joti tells you with confidence. (Keer 25.)

He went from door to door and through his poems, Phule propagated the importance of education and requested people to start schools for women and Shudras without expecting any funds to run the schools. "Light (a thousand) lamps by opening plenty of Government schools (for the Shudras' children) and illuminate the lives of the (teeming) Shudras and allied persons (in this country) without taking any aid in the form of the 'local fund' from anyone" (Patil 143).

Phule expressed his gratitude to the Britishers and expected others to do so because of their selfless contribution to spread knowledge without any discrimination and for which they opened schools in the land were the law of Manu said that it was crime to impart education / knowledge to the Shudras and women. "You should thank the English Government heartily for their kindness in having exiled (the disastrous tenants of) Manu from this land." (Patil 143)

Phule awakened the common man by saying that it was their good time now. They should change themselves by availing the opportunity. He cautioned people that the British rule would not be there forever and again they may be under the rule of orthodox people with their old system. So Phule requests people to use the opportunity.

British rule is there today. It may not be there tomorrow. It may not even outlast us. Nobody can be sure about its permanency. But as long as it is there, the lower classes should educate themselves and release themselves from the age long thralldom of brahmins which had kept them bound with ignorance and deprived them of social, personal and human dignity. (Keer 78)

Phule's deep sense of commitment to basic human values was so high that he could not tolerate injustice and atrocities in the name of religion by those who were supposed to be its custodians. In this context Phule said, "Devoid of balanced wisdom, the venerable Brahmins are truly stonehearted and following their advice is like sowing the seed of dissension." (Patil 151)

Further Phule said that if the Government took care to educate the masses there would be no difficulty in training up a body of qualified men with better 'morals and manners'. In his Memorial addressed to the Education Commission, Phule wrote to the colonial Government to open their eyes and see that more importance was given to higher education, where only people of the upper class were enjoying the funds and benefits out of it. His sincere hope was to look into the error and concentrate on primary education. He said, "My object in writing the present volume is not only to tell my Shudra brethren how they have been duped by the Brahmins, but also to open the eyes of the Government to that pernicious system of high-class education." (Patil 121)

After analyzing the inequality in the society and addressing the people Phule said that things would now improve because now God had given him the power to fight against inequality and to protect them from the evils of society. "The Lord was pleased to excite in me a desire to better their contributions through the means of education" he said. (Keer 23)

Jyotirao Phule found female literacy more necessary than male literacy because women as mothers need to give the right direction and guidance to children. This was his major contribution to female emancipation in colonial India In this context he states that before starting the school for women he first visited the missionary school at Ahmednagar to get guidance. He was impressed by the work taken up by the missionary school for the upliftment of women. "Female schools first of all attracted my notice, as upon mature consideration, they were found to be even more necessary than the male ones, the root of education lying in the proper turn mothers give to the disposition of children between their second and third years. In this state of mind I visited the school run by American Mission at Ahmednagar." (Keer 23)

Miss Farrar (belonging to the American Mission who was running a girls school in Ahmednagar), expressed to Phule and his friend Govande her displeasure at the neglect of female education in this country. They were convinced by the foreigner's perseverance in improving their country and felt for their countrymen's neglect of it. In this context Phule says, "Immediately on my return to Poona I opened a low caste female school, allowing however, such boys as wished to do so to attend also. In this I commenced to teach reading, arithmetic and the elements of grammar." (Keer 24)

For Phule education was the third eye—the instrument by which a new mode of understanding social relations could be acquired. It was as essential for low caste women as it was for low caste men. The importance of education was evident in the arguments of Phule and his colleagues. The link-up between the decline of education and the decline of people was not unique to Phule as it was a common argument of the nineteenth century reformers. What was distinctive however was the rationale for female education. While for the upper caste, exposing the punishment to women Phule showed how silly these restrictions were:

"women should forever be kept in obedience, should not be given knowledge, should not be well educated, should not know about religion(and) should not mix with men . . . women are so deprecated in support of these idiotic beliefs, and ask whether anything is written" (O'Hanlon 119)

Phule, stressing his point about the importance of education to women, questioned, "When a woman is considered a homemaker, first teacher to the child, what is it that keeps her away from knowledge?" Besides women's education, Phule's contribution to women's emancipation was twofold as mentioned earlier: abolition of sati and defense of widow remarriage. Phule tried to build a system of ideas that could look at contemporary social reality in its entirety. He took in his sweep, as any system-builder would, the past and the present.

Being a person who rebelled against injustice of any kind, Phule actively supported the movement for widow remarriage. He wanted to liberate women from their age-old shackles. In addition, while talking about the protection of women and helpless widows, Phule attempted to reduce their suffering by the burden of customs and manners. In this connection we can see the opinion of Phule on Note No. 1, by Mr. B.N. Malabari who had written an appeal to the British about 'Infant Marriage in India' and expressed the sufferings of Indian women. Phule was thankful to Malabari for bringing the pathetic condition of women to the notice of the Britishers and requesting them for help. These comments on the lawgivers with their 'malice towards female sex' are among the first gender statements in India, and flow from Phule's recognition that all women, irrespective of caste, were included among the Shudra-Ati-Shudras. Phule wrote, "I concur with Mr. Malabari laudable working and hoped something by our enlightened Government to alleviate the miserable state of the deluded people of this country. Although Mr. Malabari is under the immediate burden of our customs and manners invented by makers of Aryan Sastras, he treated the subject so remarkably well Shudra-Ati-Shudras and Brahmin widows will thank him in future." (Patil 115)

Phule, while expressing his thoughts about marriage and the suffering of women in India, gave a report to the British administration. He gave detailed information of how only a woman is targeted in the course of marriage. Whatever the reason it is the woman who is blamed and made to suffer for any conflict. Phule in a very thought-provoking way exposed the inequality meted to the girl child not even caring her age and her understanding. He explains, "In the course of marriage if any slight dispute takes place between the parties, the poor girl has to suffer all her life time. After the marriage is over, should a defect in her family happen to come to the notice of the boy's father, the innocent girl is an outcast. If the boy is younger than the girl, then the girl is not well fed, clothed and cared for properly." (Patil 115)

Phule also argues that a new bride is not brought as a wife to her husband but as a servant to the house where she is inundated with work which appeared to him harder than the lives of American slaves. The girl is more heavily loaded with work for days and nights than the American slaves. Thus she is unbearably tyrannized and obliged to end her life, and the crime is hushed up by the village Patel, Kulkarni (the quarrel monger) and policeman. (Patil 115)

To justify his point as to why women were labelled as quarrelsome, Phule found that the parents marry off children without the children's consent at a young age and when the husband grows up he develops a liking for another girl who interests him and he marries again. This is reason enough to justify women being quarrelsome. Phule gave the explanation that the reason for a woman being quarrelsome is because of the behavior of her husband who marries other women without giving her respect. She is annoyed by this and quarrels with other women: "the husband boy, on coming to his proper senses, does not like his wife and marries one of his own likings. Induced to marry two or three or four wives at a time it thus renders the whole family discontented, abusive and quarrelsome. These ignorant wives are not only obliged to poison each other, but sometimes their own husband" (Patil 115)

Phule came out with not only suggestions but also he gave remedies to handle the situations. In another appeal to the Government, Phule persuaded the Government to use compulsory measures to check the so-called higher-class Hindus holding responsible post under a Government who by their cunning and shrewd ways purposely misguided the masses in matters of religion and politics. He requested the government to bring a law to increase the marriageable age. Anyone breaking the law should be punished by imposing fine on both the parties. He also suggested that the money collected in the form of these fines should be utilized for the education of girls. In this context we find in his words: "I therefore suggest that the Government should rule that boys under eleven years of age, not marry. In case they do, the Government should levy a reasonable tax on the parents of parties married and the money thus obtained be utilized for the education of girls." (Patil 116) This was a unique idea of not only stopping marriage at a young age but also a beneficial use of the fine collected which would fund the education of middle and lower classes of Hindus.

We also get some idea of Phule's English prose style through his submissions to the Hunter Commission on Malabari's proposal. It is not as aggressive as his Marathi prose style. The way he shifts from his otherwise polemical style in Marathi to a neat, brief and to the point statement in English is admirable. A comparison between his Marathi and English writings is revealing: Marathi is aggressive, polemical and unforgiving; and English is firm, clear and relatively understated.

Phule expressed gratitude to the Scottish Mission in Poona and the Government institutions for imparting to him sound knowledge of the rights of man and above all, to British rule under which he could express his views freely and fearlessly. Expressing his thoughts on mass education, he requested the Government to be more generous in giving funds to open schools for girls. "I beg to request the Education Commission to be kind enough to sanction measures for female primary education on a more liberal scale." (Keer 179) Further Phule requested the Government sincerely, to lay more stress on primary education, for he knew it was the base of education and everyone should have the right to education. "Primary education of the masses should be made compulsory up to a certain age, say at least 12 years." (Keer 173)

When some enlightened Hindu of Bengal made excellent suggestions to university graduates he appreciated their suggestions but his point was that would not be applicable to all because very few reached university education and the remaining stopped with primary schooling itself. He further explained: "I think, their suggestions are not universal and applicable to all the classes of Shuras and Ati-Sudras, because very few of the former attend the university and the latter are not at all admitted even into vernacular schools and allowed to sit and learn." (Deshpande 194)

In one poem (Akhands), Phule expressed the importance of education and propagated: "Let all men and women labour honestly, maintain all the members of their own families honourably and thus live in joy and contentment. You should send all your children (sons and daughters) to school, and feed (helpless) students gratis. You should practice the dictates of the *Sovereign Truth* in your daily lives, and treat the handicapped persons with consideration and compassion. By such conduct you will not only make others happy and contented, but you will yourselves also be happy and contented, *says Joti*." (Patil 137)

To this and most other quotations of Phule we can apply some of the tenets suggested by Linda A. Wood and Rolf O. Kroger in the volume *Doing Discourses Analysis*. According to them a discourse has multiple possibilities: the first of these can be the reader's reaction while reading a text. Phule's speeches, writings and poems impacted the people of his generation very strongly. But there were both positive and negative responses. Today in an analysis of women's emancipation through male voices his impact has acquired a direction and focus. In this context one more parameter of Wood and Kroger can be cited, "is the context appropriate to the relationship?" (91) Phule's words to his team of social reformers has a different discourse structure than the ones where he is hitting out against radical Brahmanism. Here his own caste affiliations also come into play. When he is defending women, he uses a different tone and communication device than when he is suggesting strategies for their and society's upliftment. His writings to British officials have different discourse elements than his words addressed to Indians. These are added tools for a better understanding of his voice and vision. For instance Phule submits in Note No. II, by Mr. B.N. Malabari on 'Enforced Widowhood'. As mentioned earlier, in June 1884 a Parsi social reformer, Beheramji Merwanje Malabari, submitted to the then viceroy, Lord Ripon, two notes on child-marriage and imposed widowhood for consideration and action by the British Government. The Government forwarded these notes to the Presidency governments. It was also sent to leading personalities of the time to look into these notes which spoke of the inhuman practices. Phule was one of them. Phule reacted to the notes in a positive way with a great deal of sympathy for Brahmin widows. Talking about the ill treatment of widows, Phule vehemently opposed the shaving of heads of the widows. Moved by the sight of the shaven heads of young widows, Phule actually took out a protest rally with the barber community against the practice. He spearheaded a barbers' strike, and after that they refused to perform the customary tonsure of widows. Phule requested the Colonial Government to issue an order not to shave the heads of the widows and put an end to the physical abuse. "I most respectfully crave the favour of your enlightened English Government to remove the tyrannical system of Aryan religious institution. I therefore propose that no barber should be allowed to shave the unfortunate Brahmin widows." (Deshpande 196-97)

Phule questioned why the laws were only for a woman. If a woman did not commit sati then she was humiliated in her further life she was not allowed to remarry in spite of her being very young. Phule argues that when a woman was not permitted to remarry then it should be the same with men also. Why was it that a man could immediately get married after the death of his wife?

Not only that, he could also bring a new wife when another wife was alive. "It is quite evident from the partial Aryan religious institution that, when it prohibits the widows from remarrying, why the widowers should be allowed to remarry. If favour is shown to the latter, then the poor widows must be permitted to remarry. There is no doubt that the selfish and wicked law-givers must have addressed such unjust and non-sensical clauses into their Sastras with malice towards female sex." (Patil 118)

Further he questioned the logic of why a woman should be killed in the name of sati at the death of her husband and not a man at the death of his wife, in the name of satta (satta was of course an ironic coinage by Phule to suggest a male sati). He asked why only a woman should be blamed on her becoming pregnant for which a man was also equally responsible. Such questions are relevant even today in spite of a common understanding that women have got liberated. He said all this is because he could visualize many of women's woes to have their foundation in the wickedness of male behavior. He said, "The partial Aryan Institution inconsiderately allows polygamy to male, which causes them to fall into new habits of wickedness" (Deshpande 195)

Phule further pointed out: "Men visited prostitutes and called them *patra*, "fallen woman". They accuse women of vices but are themselves lustful, pursuing women all the time even when they are past their prime. Finally when these immortal men die, their wives will submit to the barber's hold and have their heads shaved." (Deshpande 195)

His criticism was scathing. He fearlessly and out rightly questioned the Aryans about how women felt when their husband enjoyed other woman in their presence: "But for the very few exceptional gentlemen who do not go to dances and concerts, most of the Vedic scholars, shastris, priests, reformers all being birds of the same feather are so shameless that they watch the dances of the prostitutes and their mistresses in the presence of their wives and make the dancer sit on the lap of respectable men and let her embrace each one turn by turn" (Deshpande 220)

To emphasize his point he gives a contrasting picture of the behaviour of women in hypothetical terms: "Do women ever gather together and make a young, handsome, doe-eyed, strong and robust male singer sing love songs while he gestures with his hands and shoots amorous arrows from eyes . . . and frolic with him like men do?" (Deshpande 220)

Phule was not a political reformer, but rather he was a practical reformer. He raised his voice against all religious dogmas that were unreasonable and opened the door to reforms. He aimed at reconstructing society on the basis of equality, liberty and reason.

His brief notes are significant for two reasons. One is that while Phule clarified the difference between Brahmins and Brahmanism, he advocated the smashing up of the brahmanical structure not simply because it would free the Shudra Ati Shudras, but because it would free society as a whole. Second these comments on the law-givers with their 'malice towards female sex' are pioneering gender statements in India, and arise from Phule's recognition that all women, irrespective of caste, are to be included among the Shudratishudras.

Phule not only preached but also practiced his philosophy on empowering women. He did not marry a second time for not having children in spite of pressure from his family members. He told his family to permit his wife to marry in case they wanted him to do so. He was perturbed and said, "If a pair had no child, it would be unkind to charge a woman with barrenness. It might be that the husband also was unproductive owing to his defects." (Keer 87)

Such a declaration was rare, if not unthinkable for his generation. Phule not only preached about gender equality but he also exemplified it in his own life. As thought leads to action, Phule proved in his actions that he followed what he preached. Action leads to a change in the society, Phule was successful in his goal of bringing change into society. To emphasize his point Phule questioned how a man would feel if his wife married a second husband. "If the woman went for a second husband how would her husband take it? Would he not feel insulted?" (Keer 87)

Of course, Phule was exceptional in his outright support of women. Most of the reformers at that time were merely protesting without the courage of true protestants. For instance M.G. Ranade, a noted social reformer at that time, told Phule that he had a widowed sister; Phule encouraged him to arrange for her remarriage. In his opinion: "It is the reformer's sister that is widowed. You can make the best of this sad lot. God has given you an opportunity to practice what you preach! Make bold to give effect to your vow by getting your sister remarried. No good is obtained without a struggle. Social reform does not come by itself. You have to practice it and make people accept it by your courage and suffering". (Keer 136)

But Ranade feared that his father would be deeply grieved and that Poona Brahmins would excommunicate him. Phule, in a severe retort, said angrily, *"Raosaheb, then don't pretend to be a social reformer".* (Keer 136). Again when Ranade lost his wife in October 1873, he was thirty-two and married a girl of eleven years. Phule was very angry over this act of Ranade and further said: "No good is obtained without a struggle. Social reform does not come of itself. You have to practice it and make people accept it by your courage and suffering." (Keer 136)

To make his activities of social reform take concrete shape Jyotirao Phule therefore opened a fondling home/ orphanage for orphans and widows. As noted earlier Phule and Savitribai Phule provided support even to the so-called upper caste by instituting an orphanage for the children born to Brahmin widows. The emergence of formal charitable organizations such as foundling homes/ orphanages was another pioneering effort of Phule. He did not tolerate atrocities on street orphans and widows. He was the first Hindu to set up an orphanage out of sheer pity for them. Phule condemned the Brahmins when they imposed a ban on widow remarriages. Child marriages were common among the Brahmin and other upper castes in the then Hindu society. As a result, many child widows were young and not all of them could protect themselves.

This was a decisive step in his efforts for women's emancipation. Phule gave protection to pregnant widows and assured them that the orphanage would take care of their children. He took this step when he heard of the trial of Kasi Bai, a widow's case where she was punished for killing her illegitimate baby who was illegitimate. The man behind this incident was left free and only the woman was punished. Seeing the inequality meted towards women, Phule took a resolution that he would do his best to save these women. Some of the delinquent child widows resorted to abortion or left their illegitimate children to find for themselves on the streets. This was possibly the first such institution founded by a Hindu. It was especially radical as the codes repressing women's sexuality were most strongly administered by the upper castes, so such a home would have been used largely by upper caste women. Analyzing the main reason behind the widows' sufferings, Phule came up with a solution to protect these women because he believed that it was wrong to punish only the women when the responsibility was not theirs alone. His deep sympathy made his words and actions acquire a significant dimension to the kind of discourse he employed to extend support to all women in need, irrespective of caste. As he said, "I was compelled to establish a foundling house in my own compound in Pune for the Brahmin community immediately after Kashibai's trial was over. The enclosed copies of printed notices pasted on the walls of the corners of the street where the Brahmins reside. From its commencement up to the present time thirty-five pregnant widows came to this house and delivered children of whom five are living and thirty died by the injuries inflicted by them while in the womb by the poisonous drugs which the mothers must have taken with a view to conceal their pregnancy" (Patil 118)

Jyotirao Phule was thus very successful in his unique project of opening a foundling house where most of the widows came there to deliver secretly. This shows how much need was there for this type of home for the widows. The material and sexual consequences of enforced widowhood were responsible for a large number of such young women becoming pregnant and having to hide their condition. For fear of excommunication they took cruel methods to overcome this problem to the extent of killing their own new born baby. Phule, after understanding their problem, set up an orphanage. His action was a great boon to the widows.

To educate women and increase their awareness that it is not their mistake and they should not blame themselves, Phule published hand bills, proclaiming the setting up of the orphanage to prevent infanticide. In his forthright manner he picked on one of the most vulnerable issues of the day: enforced widowhood and its consequences. With this Phule publicized the problem that the Brahmins would rather deal a customary manner using a tradition such as Ghatasphota, a symbolic death of the widow leading to the complete social boycott of the widows.

Jyotirao Phule started the foundling home for the pregnant widows to bring about a public awakening. His foresight in tackling the problems was such that he came out with the right solution. He was successful in all his acts in spite of opposition. A wonderful combination of a dreamer and a man of action, Phule resolved to find an effective method by which the dignity of human life was upheld.. Handbills advertising this bold announcement were pasted on the walls of houses in Poona. They read: "O you widows! Come and deliver here safely and secretly. Take your child or leave it here at your sweet will. The orphanage will look after it!" (Keer 86)

Jyotirao Phule attached more importance to deeds than words. This action of his was unique: a non-Brahmin boldly, humanely, benevolently, taking measures, especially for the sake of Brahmin widows, to save them from disgrace and avert the killing of embryos and children, and to save the lives of the widows who often either committed suicide or were involved in criminal proceedings. He adopted a baby boy from one such widow who had come to deliver her baby. He named the baby Yashwant, who became a doctor.

Therefore, adoption as a method for betterment of society was Phule's precept and he also demonstrated it practically. Concentrating on child abandonment, he set an example in this regard as well. He undertook in addition the bold task of teaching orphaned untouchable girls. Phule's actions were those of a visionary but they were a shock to the religious heads. Though Phule devoted considerable attention to enforced widowhood among upper caste women, women of Brahmin community in particular, he was not unconcerned about the differences among women based on caste and their place in the rituals associated with procreation.

Jyotirao Phule was more of a revolutionary. He had a complete system of ideas, and was amongst the early thinkers to have identified, in a manner of speaking, classes in Indian society. He analyzed the *dvaivarnik* structure of Indian society, and identified the Shudras as the basis of the revolution on behalf of the whole society, to liberate the entire people from the shackles of brahmanism. Phule was the thinker who thought about the complete smashing up of the entire oppressive structure, ideology and material which, according to him, was necessary and possible. Phule compared the plight of a peasant woman and that of a *bhat* woman and said that the difficulties of the peasant were more than the bhat (Phule called Brahmins as bhat) woman so he raised his voice and said, "There is rarely the ceremonial sweeping and sprinkling of water in the courtyard of a shudra's house. Nor is there the holy basil plant (Tulsi) in the courtyard. The shudra has no time for such frivolous tricks. She does not (find time to) comb her hair and her body is sticky with perspiration. She hates all finery and finicking." (Patil 111)

Extending this further Phule expressed great concern for the families of farmers and he directed the Government to watch the conduct of farmers. Phule believed that if the men of poor farmers were stopped from drinking and gambling then there would be progress in their family. If not it was the woman who suffered for she was not only humiliated by the husband for not giving him money to satisfy his addiction but also the responsibility of taking care of the family fell on her. He further said, "Those Shudras who lived immorally must be punished. They should not have more than one wife. They should not perform the marriage of their children at an early age." (Keer 190)

During the last decade of his life regarding women's oppression, Phule publicly defended both Pandita Ramabai and Tarabai Shande who opposed the Brahmin rules and the subordination of women. In Ramabai's case he went further than compatriots did to recognize women's subordination. Whatever Phule preached he was able to concretize in his lifetime itself. For example, educating women: he opened schools and also made his wife a teacher to teach the girl students. Later he noticed that educated women from the upper caste who started reading and getting to know facts opted for conversion. Some women started questioning the inequalities of women in society. While some started questioning God. And many of them expressed these views in writing. It is almost as though Jyotirao Phule gave a voice to women in addition to raising his voice in their cause. This is evident in Phule's defense of Tarabai and Ramabai contained in two articles published in *Sastar* (the essence of truth) in September and October 1885. For the preface of Satsar II which he wrote to praise Pandita Ramabai and Tarabai Shinde for their bold act Phule wrote: "These days, because of the efficacy of the English rule, a few of the harassed women are able to read and write a little. We have tried in this issue to bring to their notice how the cunning Aryan people have tortured women for thousands of years, and how they continue to do it even today. In one or two places we have admonished some of the unworthy quarrelsome sons rather harshly and we sincerely request our loving mothers and sisters to forgive us for this." (Deshpande 215)

Satsar is in dialogue form: his son Yashawant questioning and Phule clarifying his doubts. Yashawant asked a question about the many books written by the Aryans none of which contained the true meaning of the word dharma. Replying to this Phule explained: "If the books of the brahmans had true meaning of dharma and they maintained their conduct according to it then Pandita Ramabai and many other learned Brahmins would not have converted to Christianity." (Deshpande 212)

In another instance there was discussion over the topic of conversion in Satsar in the dialogue when the Brahmin tells the Shudra that they had been making special efforts towards spreading education for women. They too have condemned the prohibition of women's education following the Brama Samaj. Phule tells: "Do not say whatever comes to your mind. In fact the Hindu women are able to get education because of the efficacy of the English rule. Because of that rule, general education and the like have become quite common. Not only this but all the big and small associations established by all of you are the fruit of the education imparted by the English." (Deshpande 209)

Phule believed that when all Sudras ati shudras and women got education the Brahmins will have to leave Brahmanism. In reply the Brahman said that they would become sanyasis. They also questioned Phule about which religion he belonged to. Phule critically answers: "Forget God and serve the brahmans! Do you think this ought to be our religion? We shall adopt Christianity or Islam whenever we feel like for our convenience. Or perhaps we shall ask for a religion for us from our creator. You do not have to worry about us. But you must take care not to become a sanyasi and waste your life by opening the path of Christianity for an educated woman like Pandita Ramabai." (Deshpande 210)

Although he was vociferous in supporting women, he did not countenance either conversion or their writing negative tracts. Phule vetoed the conversion of women from one faith to another as a better option to overcome oppression. Ramabai was one such case. She received sympathy as long as she subscribed to the liberal Brahmin reformist programme. In fact, she had been something like a Gargeyi and Maitreyi come alive for those reformist Brahmans who wished for a restoration of the great golden age of the ancient past. Ramabai's conversion to Christianity was a slap in the face to all sections of the Brahmans because it was unprecedented—no woman with a public image had done so yet—and because it drew attention to a Brahmin widow's dissatisfaction not only with traditional but with reformist brahmanical society. The reaction to her conversion was hysterical: as Phule points out in the *Sastar,* even the Shudras joined the chorus: "Even before Pandita Ramabai came to Pune, Tarabai Shinde of Buldhana wrote a book called *Stree Purush Tulana.* In this book she has given excellent advice to men, for most of them behave as they will and sinfully in the presence of their women." (Deshpande 217)

The discussion went on further and Phule was told that the orthodox people's opposition to Pandith Ramabai's conversion had a reason. The question was: why were some of the Shudras opposing her conversion. Phule answered this by saying, "These days, even the great scholars and their pure equipment of worship nay with all their useless articles, having drunk the alcohol with the mlecchas brew out of rotten ingredients, our shudra and atishudra brothers still consider their drunken caste to be pious. What then is the greatness of such shudras when they call out to the brahmans saying Pandita Ramabai is unpurified when the priest sprinkled a little clean water over this chaste virtuous woman?" (Deshpande 210-11)

He further criticized an editor who wrote ill about Pandita Ramabai and said: "Had he educated his wife at home like the honourable Madhavrao Govindrao Ranade and had he then criticized Tarabai and Ramabai, the trumpet of his fame would have been heard in America. This woman-chaser does not even deserve to take Ramabai's name, for what is the extent of his understanding? Can he himself write as systematically and yet piercingly as Tarabai? If we weigh him against Pandita Ramabai he will come up short." (Deshpande 218)

Jyotirao Phule skillfully uses Ramabai's conversion to build a critique of brahmanism based on caste and gender oppression. Ramabai's critique of brahmanical patriarchy is implicitly associated with education of Brahmin women to understand their rights. Phule dwells particularly on the ambiguous position of the liberal Brahmins on inequality as well as to the inconsistency in first extolling Ramabai for her intelligence and courage and then regarding her as a *batli,* one who is fallen or impure. However, her search for a more humane system brought her closer to other oppressed people.

Throughout his two articles, in the *Sastar* Phule implicitly connects women and the Shudras as the two oppressed groups. He felt that attacks on them in the press were baseless and repressive, made only by those who gained from the subordination of women. Jyotirao Phule argues further that the allegations against women made in the press were a consequence of the envy and intolerance of women who were beginning to express themselves by articulating their views in print. Phule draws attention to the fact that the Shudras did not read to discover what was wrong with the brahmanical texts unlike the 'Arya' women who had begun to reject the text. Phule is thus acutely conscious of the relationship between knowledge and power and the need to have democratic access to knowledge to overthrow the power that its monopoly gave rise to.

Jyotirao Phule's defence of Tarabai and Ramabai became a discourse on the nature of the oppression of women and showed his understanding of women. He pointed out that only someone who had suffered could understand the nature of oppression.

Phule's book *Sarvajanik Satya Dharma Pustak* (the Book of True Faith) was an attempt at eliminating the middleman between god and man. This book therefore attempts a reformulation of the Hindu belief-system which would eliminate the priestly class, the Brahmin. This is a radical position to take even today; in 1891, it must have been more shocking still. Phule argues passionately for reforming Hinduism into a monotheistic, humane, and benevolent system. The book demonstrates the relevance of Phule and his *Sarvajanik Satya Dharma Pustak.* In this book which is also in dialogue form, in one of the articles 'Woman and Man' (Deshpande 231) he explains about the superiority of women compared to men.

The creator has created in this world sources of pleasure for both man and woman. They also enjoy each other's company. Women are self-restrained by nature. She permits a man to make friends with her. The clever man however plays upon the natural desire of the woman. Their closeness grows. . . . The patient woman carries their child without complaint. . . . Doubtless woman is superior to man." (Deshpande 231)

Phule names his books or his organization after deep thought. Like *Sarvajanik Satya Dharma Pustak* (the Book of True Faith), *Satya Shodhak Samaj* (Society for the Seekers of Truth), *Sastar* (the Essence of Truth) show how much importance was given to truth and it was because of truth he was able to oppose confidently the oppression without any fear. To convey the message of the samaj they adopted the common man's dress so that they could attract people and make them feel comfortable with them to make learning and understanding their teachings easy.

Phule convened a meeting of his followers and admirers and it was decided to form the *Satya Shodhak Samaj* (Society for the Seekers of Truth). With a rational outlook they moved to social action through their emotional involvement. Their language was the language of the people; their places of propaganda were the corn-gathering places. The dress of the preachers of the Samaj consisted of a blanket, a turban and a dhoti, and he had a drum in his hand. The topics they made poor people were aware of debts, injunctions and rites imposed on them by the cunning and selfish Brahmin priests. They urged them to send their children to schools so that they might learn about law, religion, and god. Unlike other institutes of that time, Phule's institute attempted to organize a struggle to uplift the masses. It raised its voice against social slavery and demanded social justice. It was the shrill voice of the long-suppressed people of India. Through his Samaj, Phule started translating its resolution into action. He granted scholarships to students for their education. He next changed his attention towards the religious aspect of the mission of the Samaj. He made simple rules and regulations to perform a marriage. His main purpose of doing so was to make people understand the meaning of marriage which the Brahmin priests had made complicated. When one such marriage took place, news about this marriage appeared in some newspapers under the title: "Hindu Marriage without a Brahmin Priest!" This shows how he wanted to show to the common man that a marriage is not one which has to be performed paying the priest heavy fees but it is the mutual understanding of a man and a woman, for which Phule framed some sensible rules. Understanding it and following it was the main purpose of marriage. The promises written by him described that both men and women are equal and they have to respect each other.

Phule made stirring speeches explaining the stand of the Satya-Shodhak Samaj at several villages. Phule being a man of action he performed a marriage without a Brahmin priest. News of this appeared in newspapers as 'Hindu Marriage without a Brahmin Priest'. His purpose was to convey message that people can perform marriages in a simple way as well. He wanted people to become better men, and not to waste their lives by giving huge amounts to the priest to perform marriage. The language of the samaj was the language of the people, their place of propaganda were the corn-gathering places. The dress of the preachers consisted of a blanket, a turban and a dhoti, and had a drum in their hand. Phule wanted the common man to understand his teachings in a simple way.

New activities of men of action always attracted new lieutenants: Phule was joined by a band of workers in his cause of social justice. One of the workers wrote in Dnyanodaya that since the rise of knowledge among the lower castes they knew what was proper and what was improper, what religion was and what was not. The Satya Shodhak Samaj was spreading this light. Several well-to-do and generous-minded donors were coming forward to help the movement with money, printing press, and other things. The sincerity and drive of the Satya-shodhak Samaj evoked a tribute to its workers from a journal which said that the widow remarriage institution in Bombay should take a leaf out of the Samaj's book. And it was a proper reminder to the ideologues of social reforms. The Samaj also reflected the minds of its leaders. Jyotirao Phule made speeches and gave model lessons at schools encouraging teachers to adopt better methods of teaching to keep up the interest of the children. The Samaj petitioned the Principal of the Engineering College to admit a few non-brahmin poor students free. It succeeded in its demand. This was an indication of a great change Hindu society was undergoing.

Power structure plays a very important role. Thought is action, and only action can make thought of any value. Through his actions as a practical man Jyotirao was successful in breaking the power structure which was practiced to suppress woman socially. Joti Rao Phule had truth, the invincible weapon, on his side .Thus Joti Rao's contribution to female emancipation in colonial India is more of action. Like a pathfinder his utterances and the practices that he followed are an example to others to follow.

Phule's canvas was broad, his sweep majestic. He identified and theorized the most important questions of his time—religion, the varna system, ritualism, language, literature, British rule, mythology, the gender question, the conditions of production in agriculture, the lot of the peasantry. This list, already formidable, can be extended as well. A social reformer is a liberal humanist. Phule was progressive and creative in his understanding and reactions to social structures. Later one can see Ambedkar also followed Phule in challenging the social structure which according to them was the main reason for inequality in the society.

Women in the Public Domain: Mahatma Gandhi

Today M.K. Gandhi is a globally recognized and respected voice. In matters relating not only to India but also issues concerned with total human evolution, the philosophy of Gandhi has a far-ranging impact. There are innumerable areas of social concerns that are addressed by his opinions. His presence at a crucial time in the political upheaval of India has left an indelible imprint on the country's history. And amid all this, his concern for women as equal partners in the progress of the country has brought about a decisive change in the thought process of Indians. It is therefore relevant to analyze how his discourse worked for the emancipation of women in order to free them from being restricted to the private spheres of existence and bringing them into the public domain. For this it is important to keep the backdrop of Gandhi's contemporary society in mind.

Gandhi's contribution was mostly through letters and counseling. To analyze his discourse, it is essential to look into discursive change in relation to social and cultural change; how processes of rearticulation affect orders of discourse and new gender relations. (Fairclough 1992, 96)

By the late nineteenth century, social reform movements were beginning to show their effects: although instances of personal revolt such as Pandita Ramabai's in Maharashtra were still rare, the number of women in public spheres had increased considerably. 'Celebrated women novelists' such as Nirupama Devi and Anurupa Devi were discussed in Bengali literary circles and were members of literary clubs.

Maharashtra's first woman novelist, Kashibai Kanitkar started writing in 1890, and the first woman doctor, Anandibai Joshi, qualified around the same time. Despite these signs of progress, the milieu in which such women lived was often harsh and hostile. In Punjab and Bengal, both the Arya Samaj and the Brahmo Samaj spawned women preachers leading to the consternation of many male reformers. It was in these years too that women began to get involved in nationalist campaigns and organizations, though they had to overcome a certain degree of resistance from the men surrounding them in order to do so.

In spite of such slow progress, when Gandhi emerged on the political scenario, social evils like child marriage and dowry system were rampant. The percentage of women with basic education was as low as two percent. The patriarchal nature of the society confined women to the status of a subordinate to their male counterparts. The *purdah* system was still in vogue in Northern India. Unless accompanied by their male guardians, women were not permitted to venture out on their own. Only a handful could avail of education and attend schools. It was in such a dismal milieu that Gandhi took the responsibility of shouldering a social crusade that led to a major reorientation of the common notion of women in Indian society.

The greatness of Gandhi lay in the abundance of credibility he created in the hearts of the people of India. His success always owed to the principles of love and defense of truth, utter selflessness, the importance of ways to achieve ends, courage, faith in God and renunciation. He admitted that all these principles would not be that easy to follow, but he succeeded in adopting them throughout the period of his life setting himself to be an ideal example for others. At the same time he never asked or forced others to adopt his principles in their lives.

Mohandas Karamchand Gandhi was born in Porbandar, Kathiawar, on the western coast of India. For several generations, the Gandhis had been Prime Ministers in several Kathiawar States. Karamchand Gandhi, his father, was the Chief Minister of

Porbandar and a member of the Rajasthan Court. Putlibai, Gandhi's mother, was a deeply religious Hindu. When Gandhi was sixteen, his father died – four years later he lost his mother. Gandhi later wrote in his book of memoir, *An Autobiography: The Story of My Experiments With Truth* (1927-29) “The outstanding impression my mother has left on my memory is that of saintliness.”

Gandhi was married at the age of 13, as was not unusual by the custom. His bride, Kasturba, also was 13. Kasturba could not read or write and Gandhi's attempts to teach her were fruitless. Although she often had to submit to her husband's decisions, she also had a will of her own.

In 1888 Gandhi went to London to study law, for three years. In the new surroundings he began experiments with diet that continued throughout his lifetime. After he was called to the bar at Inner Temple, he returned home to practice as a barrister in Bombay. Unable to find a suitable post, Gandhi moved to South Africa in 1893. During his journey to Pretoria he had a firsthand experience with racist degradation, a most crucial experience. In his formative years Gandhi gained fame as a tenacious political campaigner, who courageously opposed the Transvaal government's discriminatory legislation against Indian settlers. His ideological basis was much derived from the liberal-humanist values he had absorbed in England, exemplified in the works of Ruskin, Thoreau, and Emerson.

During his stay for twenty long years in South Africa, Gandhi’s life was one of prolonged struggle and suffering. He waged a relentless peaceful struggle against racial discrimination meted out to the black Indians at the hands of white South Africans. He began to teach a policy of passive resistance to and non-cooperation with the South African authorities. He derived part of the inspiration for this policy from the Russian writer Leo Tolstoy, whose influence on Gandhi was profound.

In 1914 Gandhi returned permanently to India. He became a highly influential figure in the National Congress, transforming it into an instrument of change. Following the massacre at Amritsar in 1919, in which British soldiers killed hundreds of Indians, Gandhi launched a policy of non-violent non-co-operation to secure *swaraj* (independence) from Britain. This process made Gandhi a guru-like figure. Resistance methods included strikes, refusal to pay taxes, abandonment of western attire for Indian dress, and refusal to respect colonial law.

During the freedom movement, Gandhi became the most important leader in the complex struggle being waged by people of vast diversity in temperaments, culture and language. He successfully advocated before the people the essential need for the attainment of total political independence. Soon he started a powerful campaign for home rule. During the First World War, the British colonial rulers had promised that India would be granted freedom provided Indians extended support in the war. Believing their words to be true, Gandhi supported the English army by playing an active part in recruiting soldiers. But unfortunately the British colonial rulers went back on their promise and did not grant freedom to India.

In 1936 Gandhi moved his headquarters from Sabarmati to Sevagram, a village near Wardha, which became a center to test his ideas. During World War II Gandhi's struggle for India's independence and *satyagraha* (defense of and by truth) became a threat to the war effort of the Allies. Gandhi, as a result, intensified his struggle, again advocating the *Satyagraha.* He launched the freedom movement with peace and non-violence as the only weapons. He exhorted Indians to resort to non-violent resistance to the British colonial rulers. When the Parliament passed the Rowlatt Act conferring the Indian colonial authorities with emergency powers to deal with the so-called revolutionary activities, Gandhi spread his peaceful inventive method, *Satyagraha, attracting* millions of Indians. "Nonviolence and truth (*Satya*) are inseparable and presupposes one another. There is no god higher than truth." (Saxena) The immediate response came in the form of 'Satyagraha' when the people held a peaceful demonstration against the Rowlatt Act at Jallianwala Bagh in Amritsar of Punjab province.

During the days of the freedom struggle, Gandhi visualized an idea of economic development for India. Economic independence for India involving the total boycott of British goods by the Indians was made a corollary of Gandhi's *Swaraj* movement. The *Swaraj* is derived from Sanskrit meaning "self-governing". He made a great deal of significant contributions on the economic issues of Indian society, for he found that the exploitation of Indian villagers by the British industrialists had resulted in extreme poverty in the country and the virtual destruction of Indian home industries. As a remedial measure, Gandhi advocated revival of the cottage industries. He himself set an ideal example in this. He began to use a spinning wheel as a token of the return to the simple village life he preached and the renewal of native Indian industries.

After proving his abilities of struggle, Gandhi set himself as an ideal model, practicing all the qualities that he cherished and practiced. His life of total simplicity is a classic example to all even today. He lived a simple, spiritual and ascetic life of prayer, fasting and meditation. Indians revered him as a saint and began to call him Mahatma (great soul). Gandhi's denial of the pleasures of food, sex, family, and friendship, has made his way of life extremely demanding for ordinary people, who otherwise have found inspiration from his courage and teachings.

Gandhi strongly advocated non-violence, known as *ahimsa*, 'devoid of violence'. By the pursuit of the path of non-violence by the Indian freedom fighters, Gandhi firmly believed that the British colonial rulers in India too would eventually consider 'violence' a useless weapon to suppress Indians' peaceful independence movement and would leave India.

Gandhi's influence on the Indian masses across the country and educated elite and intellectuals throughout the globe was so powerful that he became a national and international figure soon. His political and spiritual hold on India and Indians was so great the British colonial rulers in India dared not deter him from spearheading the Indian freedom movement.

Gandhi's contribution to Indian society was twofold. On the one hand, his series of campaigns for civil disobedience continued, as a result of which he was arrested twice and he fasted several times. His fasts were effective measures against the British because internal war might well have broken out had he lost his life. On the other hand, Gandhi worked for the eradication of diverse social evils like untouchability, child marriages and the oppression of women. When the British agreed to consider the untouchables as a separate part of the Indian electorate, Gandhi vehemently opposed it and undertook a fast unto death as he was opposed to the division Indian society on the basis of caste. Though himself a Hindu, he felt that it would be great injustice if his fellow brethren were made to stand on a separate political plank.

By 1944, India's struggle for freedom was in its final phase. The British Government having agreed to grant independence on the condition that the two contending nationalist groups, the Muslim League and the Indian National Congress Party, resolved their differences. Gandhi steadfastly stood against the partition of India but ultimately had to agree in the hope that internal peace would be achieved after the Muslim demand for separation had been satisfied. India and Pakistan became separate states when the British granted India independence in 1947. But the partition did not take place peacefully. Communal riots broke out causing much bloodshed. Riots engulfed Calcutta, now Kolkata, the largest of the Indian cities. Mahatma Gandhi pleaded with Hindus and Muslims and requested them to live together peacefully. He undertook a long fast until the riots ended. On January 13, 1948 Gandhi undertook another successful fast in New Delhi to bring about peace, but on January 30, 1948, twelve days after he abandoned the fast, as he was on his way to his evening prayer meeting, he was assassinated, shot with a pistol, by a fanatic Hindu, Nathuram Godse.

Gandhi helped India's struggle for independence from Britain through a campaign based on nonviolence and civil disobedience. His doctrine of nonviolent action had a profound influence on Martin Luther King Jr., the leader of the civil rights movement in the U.S, and Nelson Mandela, the most prominent figure of the black opposition to apartheid in South Africa.

The greatest contribution that Gandhi made to female emancipation was *Satyagraha* which would be based on feminist values; he also advocated a feminist strategy to achieve that ideal. Gandhi aimed at creating a non-violent society based on truth. He had mystified the concept of truth using an abstract language like his definition of truth that there is an unalterable law governing everything that exists or lives and that it was not a blind law, for no blind law can govern the conduct of living beings. For Gandhi this unalterable law was the truth. This truth was non-violence which is love.

Nevertheless, behind Gandhi's mystical explanation there is an advocacy of a society based on humanitarian values. It envisages a society free of exploitation, establishing social, political and economic equality—which would not discriminate against human beings on the basis of birth, colour, sex or nation. The basis of a society of this kind will be love, co-operation, care, sympathy, and all those virtues with which women are associated, as contrasted with the purported male qualities of coercion, selfishness or brute force. Indeed women have been denied this kind of a place in society so far. It is *sarvodaya* for all including women.

Gandhi's enunciation of a feminine strategy that is Satyagraha is a unique strategy which has never been used as a practical method of socio-political change. The remarkable feature of this society is women's participation in creating it. Prominent Gandhian Nirmala Deshpande expressed Gandhi's choice of women as his best crusaders.

Gandhi's contribution to female emancipation in the British colonial period was manifold. Primarily, Gandhi's approach towards the problem of women was always pragmatic. Gandhi's socio-political philosophy is feminist which addresses gender equity constructed on patriarchal values. There is a contradiction in them; however Gandhi based the edifice of his philosophy on this contradiction. Politics and social life have always been associated with masculinity. It is concerned with the power struggle, coercion, war, greed, selfishness, domination, bloodshed, hatred, deceit, cruelty and above all, violence. They are all masculine values which make it difficult for women to participate in it as they are not thought to be part of feminine character.

Gandhi's enunciation of a feminine strategy that is Satyagraha is a unique strategy which has never been used as a practical method of socio-political change. The remarkable feature of this society is women's participation in creating it. Gandhi explained: "Passive resistance is a method of securing rights by personal suffering; it is the reverse of the resistance by arms. When I refuse to do things that are repugnant to my conscience, I use soul force. It involves sacrifice of self. Everybody admits that sacrifice of self is infinitely superior to sacrifice of others." (Joshi 371)

As a sequel to female emancipation, Gandhi launched many struggles in India for a number of issues like untouchability, protection of cows, basic education and above all, freedom struggle. They were termed as non-cooperation movement, Civil Disobedience Movement and Quit India Movement. All these movements were completely based on his philosophy of *Satyagraha*. Its basic meaning was holding on to truth, hence truth-force. In this connection he added, "I have also called it 'love force' or 'soul force'. In the application of *satyagraha*, I discovered in the earliest stages that pursuit of truth did not admit of violence being inflicted on one's opponent but that he must be weaned from error by patience and sympathy." (Kiran Saxena)

Gandhi based his program of action not on traditional political methods. They were based on virtues, and would be suitable for women. Gandhi admitted that he had designed his strategy and chosen this particular form of struggle very consciously and deliberately so as to encourage women's participation. In his opinion, in one of his writings: "My contribution to the great problem of women's role in society lies in my presenting the acceptance of truth and ahimsa in every walk of life, whether for individuals or nations. I have hugged the hope that in this, woman will be the unquestionable leader and having thus found her place in human evolution, will shed her inferiority complex." (Kiran Saxena)

According to Gandhi, there were two major influences on the development of his concept of Satyagraha: his wife Kasturba, and his mother. "The former was a 'woman always of strong will, which in our early days I used to mistake for obstinacy. But that strong will enabled her to quit unwittingly to become my teacher in the art and practice of non-cooperation. The practice began with my own family. When I introduced it in 1906 in the political field it came to be known by the more comprehensive and specially coined name of Satyagraha." (Radha Kumar 82)

It is interesting to note here that Gandhi confessed that he had learnt the technique of non-violent passive resistance from women, especially from his wife and mother. It was Kasturba's passive resistance against Gandhi's unreasonable actions and attitudes as a man and as a husband that compelled him to change himself from the position of a dominating husband to that of an understanding husband realizing the spirit of equality and acting upon the principle of mutual consideration. He spoke of Kasturba as it is to her moral strength and example that he owed his most unique and potent idea in personal growth as well as in activist politics. He acknowledges: "I learned the lesson of non-violence from my wife, when I tried to bend her to my will. Her determined resistance to my will on the one hand, and her quiet submission to the suffering of my stupidity involved on the other, ultimately made me ashamed of myself and cured me of my stupidity in thinking that I was born to rule her." (Kiran Saxena)

Gandhi defined it as a special quality of Indian womanhood based on the woman's existence as mother. For Gandhi, the experience of pregnancy and motherhood especially qualified women to spread the message of peace and non-violence. If they could endure labour pains, they could endure anything. "I have suggested in these columns that woman is the incarnation of ahimsa. Ahimsa means infinite love, which again means infinite capacity in the largest measure. She shows it as she carries the infant and feeds it during nine months and derives joy in the suffering involved. . . . Let her transfer that love to the whole of humanity, let her forget that she ever was or can be the object of man's lust." (Forbers 26-27)

When a question was put to him about the position of women in the family, Gandhi said that wives had all the rights which husbands enjoyed. He further clarified that their duties were different but the rights were the same. He further said, the husband saying 'I am your master, you are my property, you should do as I tell you' was the kind of thing that had no place in his ideology. He said: "Satyagraha is the final weapon against such an attitude in husbands. A woman too can resort to it. It is both a single-edged and double-edged sword. It can be used anywhere with success, the husband has no alternative but to give in before this strength of love . . . she will have to walk in it and that too bare-footed, not with shoes on." (Joshi 293)

Whatever the task Gandhi was involved in, women were always participating in all the constructive activities Gandhi had undertaken. They managed various ashrams he had set up on the basis of his philosophy at Phoenix, Sabarmati and Sevagram. Besides his wife, many distinguished women like Sarojini Naidu, Sushila Nayar, Amrita Kaur, Suchetha Kriplani, et al., were his associates. Because he was of the opinion: "She will occupy her proud position by the side of man as his mother, maker and silent leader. It is given to her to teach the art of peace to the warring world thirsting for that nectar. She can become the leader in Satyagraha which does not require the learning that books give but does require the stout heart that comes from suffering and faith." (Forbers 26-27)

Gandhi said that only women could fight militarism. In Italy he said in one of his speeches, "I have no doubt that they can do infinitely more than men against war." (Joshi 259) He elaborated his argument to the gathering there that it is the woman who in spite of her suffering accepts the man going to war and takes care of the family. It is because of this that a man can boldly participate in war. So according to Gandhi women are stronger than men; the only thing is that she is behind the screen. He said to the audience, "Answering for yourselves what your great soldiers and generals would do, if their wives and daughters and mothers refused to countenance their participation in militarism in any shape or form in militarism." (Joshi 259)

In fact, Gandhi's advocacy of non-violence created favourable conditions for mass participation of women in all the movements he launched. They came out of their houses instead of hiding in fear, as they usually did when the movements were violent. S*atyagraha* made women feel that because of their femininity they are not inadequate or inferior to men. They were made to understand that their femininity was not downgraded because their propensity to face violence is considered less, but they are strong because of their feminine character.

As regards women's role in non-violent movements, speaking to a group of women in Italy, Gandhi said: "The beauty of non-violent war is that women can play the same part in it as men. In a violent war women have no such privilege and Indian women played a more effective part in our last non-violent war than men. The reason is simple. Non-violent war calls into play suffering to the largest extent and who can suffer more purely and nobly than women". (Joshi 259)

Violence must be avoided to the extent possible but when it becomes the honour of self or the nation, then one must be ready to face the enemy. Gandhi stressed on non-violence and said: "Touching upon non-violence, if some maniac should try to assault a woman, and if another man should happen to be present, should he not protect her honour with the use of a weapon? Should not women train themselves in the use of weapons and learn to protect themselves? I have given my opinion. Use of a weapon would certainly imply violence but I have never permitted anyone to draw from this the inference that a man or woman who happens to be present should not run to the rescue of the woman and should tolerate an outrage on her modesty." (Joshi 277)

Gandhi explained to men that if they allow the modesty of a woman in the name of non-violence then it means he has not understood non-violence properly. He advises men to take care of women when they are in need. Those are the qualities of heroism. "I have said that the man who allows the modesty of a woman to be thus outraged will be regarded as a coward. He will be a partner in violence because violence is less sinful than cowardly violence. A heroic man or woman can learn the lesson of non-violence, it is pretty nearly impossible for a coward to learn it." (Joshi 277)

Gandhi further explains to the *ashram* women in detail about protection of oneself by using a weapon like a dagger may not help because if anyone takes away the dagger then it will be very difficult for her to protect herself. She should use soul-force and slap him. He explained: "Their slap is not an expression of violence, only of their opposition. . . . Hence her act is not violence; but it is a power to move a lecherous mind and to awaken the woman who administers the slap." (CWMG 1944, 17-19)

Gandhi's autobiography continues to give vent to his feelings, besides the customs of child marriages, on such other social evils like Purdah, when he says, "The Purdah was vicious, brutal and barbarous." He further explained how the women in India abandoned the practice of *purdah*, which was a punishment to the women in the name of religion. Gandhi very proudly exclaimed that with his call for independence the Indian women came out of their purdah and were ready to face the British people to get independence. This was a heroic act which Gandhi expressed to the foreign women about the Indian woman. "The women in India tore down the purdah and came forward to work for the nation. They saw that the country demanded something more than looking after their homes. They manufactured contraband salt, they picketed foreign cloth shops and liquor shops and tried to wean both the seller and the customer from both. At late hours in the night, they pursued the drunkards to their dens with courage and charity in their hearts. They marched to jails, and they sustained lathi blows as few men did." (Joshi 259)

He further justified his point on *purdah* in *Young India*: "Chastity is not a hot-house growth. It cannot be protected by the surrounding wall of the *purdah*. It must grow from within, and to be worth anything it must be capable of withstanding every unsought temptation." (Ray 407)

Talking about the importance of the women of India compared with that of the west Gandhi said Indian women are superior when compared with women of other countries. In other countries women compare and compete with men in becoming beasts but in India women are not so. "If the women of the west will try to vie with men in becoming brutes, they have no lesson to learn from the women of India. They will have to cease taking delight in sending their husbands and sons to kill people and congratulating them on their valour." (Joshi 259)

Gandhi's role in female emancipation in colonial rule can also be seen in the crusade he had launched against anti-women religious practices. Despite his unflinching confidence in women, he never failed in realizing the real situation of women in India. He recognized that the unjust social structure, anti-women religious practices, certain rituals and conventions depicting women have marginalized women and made them victims of inhuman cruelty. Gandhi wanted the cessation of that cruelty. He worked for an end to their marginalization. In this connection he wrote in his autobiography *The Story of My Experiments with Truth:* "I have also had a passion to serve womankind. Ever since my arrival in India, the women have recognized me as their friend and servant. Women have come to look upon me as one of themselves." (CWMG 235-36)

Gandhi advised the Ashram women to write letters to him at least once a week. He said to them that they should meet regularly in the ashram to qualify themselves to get weekly letters from him and to reply to them. In this way they can improve their collective living and also they can share their thoughts and clarify doubts. In one such letter Trivenibehn asked a question: why women, not only in the ashram but all women with whom she has come in contact, looked as if they were dead and had no spirit in them at all. For which Gandhi replied: "There is some truth in her description, though of course it will not apply to all women. The reasons which I have been able to discover are these: Lack of order in women's life, Excessive worries, Wrong upbringing, Adoption of unscientific measures at the time of childbirth and during confinement. . . . In many cases, harmful thoughts which they do not try to regulate wisely but repress." (Joshi 265) He further says, "I have observed one great defect in our women, namely, that they hide their thoughts from the world. As a result, their behaviour becomes hypocritical . . . throughout their lives it eats them up like a cancer. At every step they do things which they dislike in their hearts and believe that they must do them." (Joshi 265) He advises them: "If they only think a little, they will realize that they need not let themselves be suppressed by anybody in the world. If they learn this first lesson and cultivate the courage to stand before the world just as they are, they will be able to eliminate the other causes which I have mentioned." (Joshi 265)

Gandhi in every possible way was advising the Indian women and encouraging their moral confidence. Gandhi was a confidence-builder among women. He encouraged them to participate in all the activities without feeling inferior; he, like a father, explained things to them. But simultaneously he also said that women are their own destiny-makers. They themselves have to make them strong. "I hold radical views about the emancipation of women from their fetters which they mistake for their adornment. . . . My experience has confirmed the views that the real advancement of women can come only through their own efforts." (Gandhi 1954, 235-36)

Gandhi developed a great insight into man-woman relationship ensuring women's total equality. Gandhi's utterances for female emancipation can be seen to arise from his critical study of Indian social order. He found that the treatment meted out to women in this social order is fundamentally discriminatory. Gandhi strived at ending the inhuman treatment of women.

Gandhi preached equality and also practiced the same. This can be seen in his Ashrams where experiments were carried out and also they achieved success. Work distribution was equal among women and men. Gandhi explained: "Women in the Ashram are not subject to any restriction which is not imposed on the men as well. They are placed on a footing of absolute equality with the men in all activities. Not a single Ashram task is assigned to the women to the exclusion of the men." (Joshi 274)

Talking about the independence women had in the Ashram, Gandhi further writes that, "there is no such thing as *Purdah* or *Laj* in the Ashram' (Joshi 270) Also he further said that all his preachings were implemented in the Ashram. He further said, "Women cannot make any progress so long as there are child marriages. All girls are supposed to be in duty to marry and that too before menstruation commences and widow remarriage is not permitted . . . when they join the Ashram, are told that these social customs are wrong . . . they are not shocked as they find the Ashram practicing what it preaches." (Joshi 274)

Gandhi also like other reformers found fault with the *Smritis,* but he put his argument differently. He was aware of the fact that *Smritis* bristled with contradictions and did not analyze the root cause of those contradictions and in a peripheral way struck to the half-truth that legislation has been mostly the handiwork of man, and man has not always been fair and has been discriminatory in performing that self-appointed task. The largest part of our effort in promoting the regeneration of women should, therefore, be directed towards removing those blemishes which are represented in our *shastras* as the necessary ingrained characteristics of women. Here Gandhi puts the blame on men who wrote the *shastras* and not the patriarchal system, whose ideology instructs the mind of men and women, which is articulated in the religious, social and traditional culture. Gandhi respected the traditions of society, but not at the cost of loss of individual dignity. He never hesitated to criticize the evils which had gripped Indian society, and tried to mobilize public opinion against such evils. He realized that there were deep-rooted customs hampering the development of women, and women's freedom from such shackles was necessary for the emancipation of the nation.

Gandhi often presented ideals before women, drawn from Indian traditions, mythology and history. He often talked about Sita, Draupadi, Damayanti and Mirabai as great women. There was nothing new in a social reformer drawing inspiration from tradition. What was new here was the fact that he put forth an innovative interpretation of these characters. This gave a glimpse of the dynamic element in his thinking. He did not accept the negative elements of the Hindu tradition. He visualized the Indian women as new Sitas, Draupadis and Damayantis, "pure, firm and self-controlled". To explain to the common people the greatness of the Indian women Gandhi observed that experiences had added force to the argument. "After all, who protected Sita from Ravana? The poet tells us that her purity was such that Ravana dared not compass his end without her consent." (Joshi 334) Women understood what he was saying because he spoke in the religious pantheon and referred to the facts of caste and gender. Sometimes highly progressive, other times conservative, he created an empathy with his audience through this cultural fine-tuning.

Gandhi found 'for women a new dignity in public life, a new confidence, a new self-view' concluding that 'from passive objects women became active subjects or agents of reform'. (Madhu Kishwar 9) Gandhi's definition of women's nature and role was deeply rooted in the Hindu patriarchy, and he was mostly inclined to limit the women's movements rather than push it forward.

Though he spoke of how impressed he was by the qualities displayed by women in the South African *satyagrahas,* it took many years of pressurizing from the women in nationalist movements before he was to appeal to women to join in public campaigning. In the early years, he consigned the 'special role' of women to the home: if, on the one hand, he turned the private area of the family into an arena for women's public action through emphasizing the importance of the family as a site for social change, he also, on the other hand, made it clear that further expansion of their role into the field of public action, was wrong because the art of bringing up the infants of the race is women's social and sole prerogative. In this connection, Gandhi, in one of his discourses to a group of women, emphasizes the reproductive role over other roles. Since the woman is the mother and the keeper of hearth, she is exhorted to keep off from public life. Politics and public life were to be, by and large, exclusively male domains. Gandhiji asserted, "And you sisters, what would you do going to Parliament? Do you aspire after the collectorship, commissionership or even viceroyalty? You would not care for the Viceroy to have to order executions and hangings, a thing you would heartily desist." (Kiran Saxena)

With reference to the duties of women Gandhi said: "The duty of a woman is to look after what in English is called the hearth and home. Man has never performed this task. He has been content to build forts and ramparts for protection. Will he come forward to protect the Home?...Hence it is my confirmed opinion that women should get a distinct kind of education. . . . This does not imply that the work of the one is inferior while that of the other is superior; the spheres of the two are complementary." (Joshi 294)

Gandhi was not only a great political leader but also a passive lover of humanity. An implacable enemy of all injustice and inequalities, he was a friend of the lowly and the downtrodden. Harijans, women and the poor commanded his most tender attention. He had an almost instinctive understanding of women and their problems and had a deep abiding sympathy for them. In a letter written to Raj Kumari Amrit Kaur from Wardha on October 20,

1936. Gandhi writes: "If you, women, only realize your dignity and privilege and make full sense of it for mankind, you will make it much better than it is. But man has delighted in enslaving you and you have proved willing slaves till the slave and holders have become one of the crimes on degrading humanity. My special function from childhood, you might say, has been to make women realize her dignity. I was once a slave holder myself but Ba proved an unwilling slave and thus opened my eyes to my mission." (CWMG 240)

Gandhi strived for the awakening of women, which made them shed their deep-rooted sense of inferiority and rise to dignity and self-esteem. For Gandhi the woman whom we all call *abala* should become *sabala,* all those who are helpless should become powerful. Gandhi expounds this theme further. More often than not a women's time is taken up not by the performance of essential domestic duties, but in catering to the egoistic pleasure of her lord and master. He explains: "To me this domestic slavery of woman is the symbol of our barbarism mainly. It is high time that our womankind was freed from this incubus." (King 330)

According to him, domestic work ought not to be taking the whole of women's time. His policy of empowerment was that a man must also participate in the housework and reduce the drudgery of women's work at home.

Talking about other evils like the custom of child marriage, Gandhi was of the opinion that the custom of child marriage is both a moral and a physical evil, for it undermines our morals and induces physical degeneration. Gandhi questioned the basis of the practice of pushing women into seclusion. He vehemently asks, "Why is there all this morbid anxiety about female purity? Have women any say in the matter of male purity? We hear nothing of women's anxiety about male chastity? Why should men arrogate to themselves the right to regulate female purity? It cannot be superimposed from without it is a matter of evolution from within and, therefore, of individual self effort." (Joshi 152)

Gandhi calls prostitution a sin and looks down on the men who have to enjoy have made this into a profession where they can earn money. He described it as a disease which was seen as a very dangerous one by the people at that time. To increase the impact he called it moral leprosy and despises the fact that the beast in man has made detestable crime a lucrative profession. He appealed to prostitutes to give up their unworthy profession and become *sanyasins* of India. When, in 1925, the Bengal Congress Committee organized some women prostitutes under the banner, Gandhi was almost hysterical with rage. The women had been asked to use their wages for 'humanitarian' work such as helping the poor, nursing, promoting *khadi* spinning and weaving. He exclaimed that all that money, given to him however, was ashes and dust. Gandhi requested women to give up their wage-earning work of prostitution. He exclaimed, "These women were worse than an 'association of known thieves', for they stole 'the virtue of society'. Only through reforming themselves, taking to the charkha and khadi, and welcoming suffering and self-denial, could they be accepted." (Kishwar 7)

Gandhi requested the prostitutes to stop this type of earnings because that was making them out-caste in society. He not only told them the act was wrong but he also knew that it is difficult for them to survive without money. He not only opposed the acts but showed them the remedy. He suggested to the prostitutes that they need not long for a luxurious life they should live a simple life, without greed for ornaments. He told them that the women in his ashrams had left all those things in spite of their earlier affluent condition. So he advised them, "We have discovered the spinning-wheel, which is our kamadhenu. I would not be satisfied even with you sisters taking up spinning. You should learn to weave and card as well. If you do, you will be able to earn all you need for a living." (Joshi 85)

Gandhi opposed the ancient custom of sati. He found that in the name of tradition many women were killing themselves. To utilize their services Gandhi explained to them that it is good to be chaste but killing oneself is not correct; instead they can serve the country. Gandhi had found that women adhered more closely to his creed of non-violent war, for it called into play suffering to the largest extent; he found that woman could suffer more purely and nobly than man. This emphasis on the need for, and virtue of suffering was central to Gandhi's thought: his ideal activist was the 'voluntary widow', who was a 'gift to humanity', for she had 'learnt to find happiness in suffering'. She was a true s*ati*; not the woman who burnt herself on the pyre: "A sati has been described by our ancients, and the description holds good today, as one who, ever fixed in her love and devotion to her husband, signalizes herself by her selfless service during her husband's lifetime as well as after, and remains absolutely chaste in thought, word and deed . . . she would prove her satihood not by mounting the funeral pyre at her husband's death, but she would prove it with every breath that she draws from the moment that she plighted her truth to him at the saptapadi ceremony, by her renunciation, sacrifice, self-negation and dedication to the service of her husband, . . . identifying herself with her husband (she would) learn to identify herself with the whole world." (Gandhi 247-48)

Gandhi's view of marriage as a sacrament meant that he disapproved of arranged marriages on the bases of monetary settlements or dowries, or on the ground of caste. He also strongly disapproved of child marriages and drew his own experiences, fully documented in his autobiography, to show the folly of such an institution. He regarded it as a cruel custom and considered it disgraceful that it should be given religious sanction. He remarked: "But Brahmanism that can tolerate untouchability, virgin widowhood, spoliation (sic) of virgins, stinks in my nostrils. It is a parody of Brahman therein. Child marriage ought to be abolished. This could mean that there would be fewer widows . . . but the same custom did not apply to men." (Ray 257-58)

Once a bereaved friend wrote a letter to Gandhi describing the plight of a 17 years old girl who had lost her husband, two-year old child, her father-in-law and her brother-in-law in Quetta. She returned to her mother in Lahore. The question before them was what was to be done next because some suggested a second marriage but most opposed it. So he wanted to know from Gandhi what he would suggest. Gandhi replied: "I do not know what my pen or voice can do in matters in which age-long prejudices are concerned. I have repeatedly said that every widow has as much right to remarry as every widower. Voluntary widowhood is a priceless boon in Hinduism; enforced widowhood is a curse. And I very much feel that many young widows if they were absolutely free, not so much from the fear of physical restraint as from the opprobrium of Hindu public opinion, would remarry without the slightest hesitation . . . the girls who may have become widows in the natural course will also find it easy to get married if they are willing to do so." (Joshi 295)

Gandhi considered this to be an indictment of the customs of Hindu society and he advocated, on the basis of sex equality, that widows be given the right to remarry if they so desire. He further said: If we would be pure, if we would save Hinduism, we must rid ourselves of this poison of enforced widowhood. (Ray 258) Looking at the pathetic condition of the widows in India Gandhi suggested that they come out of the old tradition of suffering, for India needs their services. He requested them to come out of the life of suffering by taking the help of the spinning-wheel: "The spinning-wheel is the life-support of a widow, a companion of any forlorn woman and now it must be a dear friend of every self-respecting Indian lady." (Joshi 89)

Gandhi's contribution to female emancipation sprang from his political awakening of women. Gandhi revolutionized not only Indian politics, but also the whole perception of life for women. In his autobiography he writes: "On the one hand, women became aware of their inner strength, and on the other, the process brought human and moral elements into politics." (Gandhi 127)

Gandhi had full faith in the role of women in getting independence from the British. Also he felt that the social evil which was prevailing in the country that is untouchability could also be eradicated with the help of women. He wrote to Janaki Devi Bajaj on September 19, 1932: "All women will have to come out of their homes as dedicated workers and eradicate the practice of untouchability and so prove their claim to be incarnations of God's powers." (Joshi 283)

Gandhi expressed his happiness when he saw the people in the Ashram expressed their desire to acquire knowledge. But there were not many teachers to teach them. In this context Gandhi said: "The superstition that no education is possible without a teacher is an obstacle in the path of educational progress. A man's real teacher is himself . . . therefore what adults need is not so much a school as a thirst for knowledge, diligence and self-confidence." (Joshi 274-75)

Gandhi offered self-confidence to women in his "war" against British domination of India. It brought them out in their hundreds from sheltered homes, to stand the furnace of a fiery trial without flinching. It seemed to prove convincingly that a woman was as able as a man to resist evil or aggression. Women could play a significant part in the freedom fight under his inspiring leadership, his fostering care and loving guidance. Therefore he said, "In this non-violent warfare, their contribution should be much greater than men's." (Joshi 222)

The women found in him not just a "Bapu", father, but what is more precious, a mother, in whose all-embracing and understanding love all fear and restraint vanish. Women shared all their problems with him including the ones related to health. For instance, in one of the letters written to Sharda C. Shah Gandhi suggests: "you must take complete rest during the period . . . if you are after it and take the treatment I am suggesting, you are sure to get well. There are natural differences between males and females. Hence, their functions too are somewhat different. This being the case, if a man tries to perform the functions of a woman or a woman that of a man, there is bound to be trouble." (Joshi 283-4)

Gandhi felt that the only factor that would enable women to come out of this situation was the determination and strength of women themselves. Though men should help in the cause of women, ultimately women will have to determine their destinies. But in the process of emancipation of women some were taking wrong steps. Gandhi expressed his contrary views of what swaraj / emancipation of women means to him. Gandhi sympathized with women, but he did not want to pity them all the time. Neither did he want them to be irresponsible, pleasure-loving beings. He had known educated girls who thought nothing of marrying men having a living wife. He called this degradation of womanhood. Such views could not be defended under the pretense of banishing social superstitions or vice. In a speech at Borivali Camp he said, "there was at present a woeful deterioration of moral standards in society among men. Even those who talked loudly about enforcing monogamy through law did not practice it themselves . . . The same tendency was beginning to manifest itself among women. Did the emancipation of women mean that they should imitate men in that respect? Certainly, India could never win swaraj, certainly not the swaraj of his conception, by following this path." (Joshi 331)

Talking about 'Modern Girl' some girls wrote to Gandhi about his comment on the modern girls with the caption 'Students' Shame which was published in *Harijan* on 31st December 1938. They said in the days when women were coming out of closed doors to help men and take an equal share of the burden of life, it was strange that they were still blamed even when they were maltreated by men. The modern girl had provoked Gandhi to the extent that he had disposed of her finally as one playing Juliet to half a dozen Romeos. They commented that his remarks which betrayed his idea about women in general were not very inspiring. For this Gandhi wrote: "My regard for the fair sex is too great to permit me to think ill of them . . . the 'modern girl' has a special meaning. Therefore there was no question of my restricting the scope of my remarks to some. But all the girls who receive English education are not modern girls. I know many who are not at all touched by the 'modern girl' spirit. But there are some who have become modern girls. My remark was to warn India's girl students against copying the 'modern girl' and complicating a problem that has become a serious menace." (Joshi 310-11)

Though Gandhi never challenged the traditional set up, he inspired women to carve out their own destinies within it, and thereby change its very essence. Women learned from Gandhi that one can be strong enough, even if seemingly weak, to protest against injustice. They realized that they do not have to accept the norms of male-dominated politics. They evolved their own perspectives and formulated their own methods. In a way, they presented a critique of the colonial unethical state.

As far as the economic emancipation of women was concerned, Gandhi felt that men and women had different spheres of work. In his opinion, women could take to economic activities like spinning, to supplement the income of their families, which he believed to be a good option available to women. And yet, there is something in his ideas that is essentially radical. He did not see women as helpless objects to be reformed. Neither did he think of bringing change only in some spheres of life, such as marriage or education. His vision of change was comprehensive. He connected the moral with the political, the social and the economic, presenting an eclectic view of life. For him the means had to be identified with the ends; similarly, he did not differentiate between the private and the public worlds of women. He also enhanced the dignity of women's housework, advising his men followers to take to spinning and to do ordinary work in everyday life. He himself imbibed so many qualities of women that he became a 'mother' to many. "I am the only one whom you may find it hard to get rid of, for I have always counted myself as a woman. I believe, I know your sex and your needs better than you do yourselves." (Joshi 339)

Gandhi had tremendous faith in women's inherent capacity for non-violence. And his experience of participation by women in politics from his days in South Africa, till the end of his life bears testimony to the fact that they never failed his expectations. With Gandhi's inspiration, they took the struggle right into their homes and raised it to a moral level. Women organized public meetings, sold *Khadi* and prescribed literature, started picketing shops of liquor and foreign goods, prepared contraband salt, and came forward to face all sorts of atrocities, including imprisonment and inhuman treatment by police officers. They came forward to give all that they had—their wealth and strength, their jewellery and belongings, their skills and labour—as sacrifices for this unusual and unprecedented struggle.

Gandhi was successful in making women participate in the public field because of his involvement in the work along with women. He advised them in simple language and sometimes took translators who translated his ideas to common women. This act of his gave him the strength and confidence to give suggestions to people. This made it easy for the illiterate people to understand what he said and this became his weapon of success to convince even an ordinary person. His language was simple and as a communicator he was easily understood by the general public. This quality of his made him a mass attractor and a national leader.

Gandhi was indeed one of the greatest advocates of women's liberty and throughout his life toiled relentlessly to improve the status of women in this country. His faith in their immense capabilities found expression in his decisions to bestow leadership to them in various nationalistic endeavours.

Gandhi's realism follows from his reading of power as unavoidable, dangerous and coveted. For him, power needs to be understood more expansively than it generally is, not to repackage in new containers that deny its hazards or inevitability, but to show people its many locations and forms. Although Gandhi does not hold the bleak view of conventional realists that people are constantly driven by ambition and are ready to dominate others, he finds that any society is open to this possibility. For this reason, Gandhi wants to domesticate power by dispersing it throughout society to avoid monopolistic or oligopolistic concentrations.

The Gandhian movement resolved the tension beautifully by retaining the religious content of nationalism while turning women an embodiment of the Shakti, a violent power, into a nonviolent one and imparting it a gentle, patient, long-suffering, sacrificial ambience particularly appropriate for women. If the movement is non-violent then no dangerous, aggressive note is imparted to the feminine personality through participation. The downside to this form a feminist perspective was that this militancy failed to mount any challenge to the institution of patriarchy.

Addressing a meeting he called for the women of India to join hands with men because he believed that if they did cooperate it would be difficult for men to fight individually. Here we can see that he builds confidence in them and also he shows them they are equal to men and also powerful. He explains to them if they don't work together the work would be incomplete. "Just as a man, with one half of his body inactive, could not do anything properly, so the Indian body would not be able to do its work properly if one half of it, namely, the women, remained inactive and so he would appeal to his sisters of India to join the satyagraha movement in large numbers." (Joshi 22)

Gandhi understood that until the women of India joined the freedom movement, it was not possible for them to win independence from the Britishers. So he called on women in most of the meetings and said if the women do not share in men's tasks, the country is bound to remain in a wretched state. Gandhi showed so much of confidence in women that in one of his speeches he said, "So long as women in India do not take equal part with men in the affairs of the world and their religious and political matters, we shall not see India's star rising." (Joshi 22)

Gandhi described discrimination against women as an anachronism. He said: "I fail to see any reason for jubilation over the birth of a son and for mourning over that of a daughter. Both are God's gifts. They have an equal right to live and are equally necessary to keep the world going." (Ray 252) Gandhi gave a clarion call to women: "Refuse to the slave of your own whims and fancies, and the slaves of men. Refuse to decorate yourselves, don't go in for scents and lavender waters; if you want to give out the proper scent, it must come out of your heart, and then you will captivate not man, but humanity. It is your birthright. Man is born of woman; he is flesh of her flesh and bone of her bone. Come to your own and deliver your message again." (Ray 258-59)

Gandhi received the same love and respect from the English women when he was in England. Just as the Indian women had not kept any secret from me even in England women came out and opened their hearts to him. They used to accompany him on his morning walks and discuss various topics with him. The moral that Gandhi drew from this is that non-violence is a very wide thing. It includes absolute freedom from impure thoughts. Not only that some of them had come to India to serve the people and to follow Gandhi. We can see Gandhi talking about some of their contributions in a letter to the Ashram women thus: "The sacrifices made by some women are beyond praise. Muriel Lester who came to stay with us at the Ashram is a daughter of rich parents. Like Mirabehn, she has given away, as a trust to the Ashram founded by her, all her share of the parental wealth. She and her sister Doris have dedicated their all to public service. Doris runs a school for children." (Joshi 261)

Gandhi scorned the extremist nationalists' attempts to revive a 'male' vigour in India as a counter to the masculinity of British colonialism. In his opinion, this could lead only to violence and hatred. He preferred to stress the 'female' principle of non-violence. Ashish Nandy has argued in this respect that Gandhi 'rediscovered' womanhood as a civilizing force in human society.

Gandhi's approach to the question of women's emancipation was one that, on the whole, he shared with many male nationalists and social reformers of his day. He held ideas such as women should receive education, should not be married off early and should be allowed to remarry if widowed. He deplored the practice of seclusion and a rigid separation of the sexes. He believed that women were biologically more suited to a life in the home. The Gandhian movement stood out for the way in which it allowed many women in India to gain a new sense of empowerment.

Experience to Achievement: Dr. B.R. Ambedkar

Ambedkar's contribution to the issue of women's emancipation and the specialized discourse he employs can be analyzed within the framework of the three dimensions of discourse mentioned by Teun A. Van Dijk: "(a) language use, (b) the communication of beliefs (cognition) and (c) interaction in social situations" (1997: 2). His caste and political affiliations have a significant role to play in shaping his beliefs, have a significant role to play in shaping his beliefs, finding expressions for them and finally communicating them to a society which invested him with a voice of authority. Therefore his voice was a crucial one to translate emancipation into actual expression.

Dr. Ambedkar appeared on the social and political scene of pre-independent India at a very crucial time when British colonialism had already created a strong sense of nationalism in the minds of millions of patriotic Indians. Ambedkar strongly believed that political independence for India would be totally meaningless without ensuring individual liberty, economic equality and political fraternity.

The seminal contribution to the history of modern India by Dr. Ambedkar, author of the Indian constitution and champion of human rights, is undisputed. He has left an indelible imprint on the political, legal, social and even the spiritual scene of modern India. In the words of his biographer, Dhanajay Keer: "Ambedkar belongs to the men of first eminence of our age. He belongs to the line of those who have been saviours of the suppressed and the oppressed. He shaped the life of sixty million people. He made his mark on the times. He wrote his name on the future of this country, and in the history of human freedom." (Keer 1962: 524)

Bhimrao Ambedkar was born on April 14, 1891 in Mhow (presently in Madhya Pradesh). He was the fourteenth child of Ramji and Bhimabai Sakpal Ambavedkar. B.R. Ambedkar belonged to the "untouchable" Mahar Caste. His father and grandfather served in the British Army. In those days, the government ensured that all the army personnel and their children were educated and ran special schools for this purpose. This ensured good education for Bhimrao Ambedkar, which would have otherwise been denied to him by the virtue of his caste.

Bhimrao Ambedkar experienced caste discrimination right from childhood. After his retirement, Bhimrao's father settled in Satara, Maharashtra. Bhimrao was enrolled in the local school. Here, he had to sit on the floor in one corner outside the classroom and teachers would not touch his notebooks. In spite of these hardships, Bhimrao continued his studies and passed his Matriculation examination with flying colours in 1908. Bhimrao Ambedkar joined the Elphinstone College for further education. In 1912, he graduated in Political Science and Economics from Bombay University and got a job in Baroda.

In 1913, Bhimrao Ambedkar lost his father. In the same year the Maharaja of Baroda awarded a scholarship to Bhim Rao Ambedkar and sent him to America for further studies. Bhimrao reached New York in July 1913. For the first time in his life, Bhimrao was not discriminated against for being a Mahar. He immersed himself in studies and attained a Master of Arts degree. In 1916 he got a Doctorate in Philosophy from Columbia University for his thesis "National Dividend for India: A Historical and Analytical Study." From America, Dr. Ambedkar proceeded to London to study economics and political science. But the Baroda government terminated his scholarship and called him back.

The Maharaja of Baroda appointed Dr. Ambedkar as his political secretary. But no one would take orders from him because he was a Mahar. Bhimrao Ambedkar returned to Bombay in November 1917. With the help of Shahu Maharaj of Kolhapur, a sympathizer of the cause of the upliftment of the depressed classes, Ambedkar started a fortnightly newspaper, the *Mooknayak* (*Dumbs' Hero*) on January 31, 1920. The Maharaja also convened many meetings and conferences of the "untouchables" which Bhimrao addressed. In September 1920, after accumulating sufficient funds, Ambedkar went back to London to complete his studies. He became a barrister and got a Doctorate in science.

One of the documents in the B.R. Ambedkar archive at Columbia University is a statement submitted by America's first Ambedkar scholar, Professor Eleanor Zelliot entitled, "Dr. Ambedkar and America". She writes, "Ambedkar was one of the first (and one of the few) Indian leaders to be educated in the United States. I am not sure what influence his years at Columbia University in New York City had on his life, but I know we can be proud to claim some part of this remarkable man's early development. Two of the qualities which marked his life and career—optimism and pragmatism—may have been enhanced by his contact with this country, which prides itself on its characteristics of hope and practicality." (Zelliot 79)

After completing his studies in London, Ambedkar returned to India. In July 1924, he founded the Bahishkrit Hitakarini Sabha (Outcastes Welfare Association). The aim of the Sabha was to uplift the downtrodden socially and politically and bring them to the level of the others in Indian society. In 1927, he led the Mahad March at the Chowder Tank at Colaba, near Bombay, to give the untouchables the right to draw water from the public tank where he burnt copies of *Manusmriti* publicly.

In 1929, Ambedkar made the controversial decision to cooperate with the all-British Simon Commission which was to look into setting up a responsible Indian Government in India. The Congress decided to boycott the Commission and drafted its own version of a constitution for free India. The Congress version had no provisions for the depressed classes. Ambedkar became more skeptical of the Congress's commitment to safeguard the rights of the depressed classes.

While Ambedkar went as a representative of the depressed classes he was conscious also that he was representing India. On the eve of his departure to England, Ambedkar said, "As regards myself, I will demand what is rightful for my people and I will certainly uphold the demand for Swaraj." The Round Table Conference was inaugurated by the King-Emperor who concluded his address: "May your names go down to history as those of men who served India well" (Keer 145) When a separate electorate was announced for the depressed classes under Ramsay McDonald 'Communal Award', Gandhiji went on a fast unto death against this decision. Leaders rushed to Dr. Ambedkar to drop his demand. On September 24, 1932, Dr. Ambedkar and Gandhiji reached an understanding, which became the famous Poona Pact. According to the pact the separate electorate demand was replaced with special concessions like reserved seats in the Regional Legislative Assemblies and Central Council of States.

Dr. Ambedkar attended all the three Round Table Conferences in London and forcefully argued for the welfare of the "untouchables". Meanwhile, the British Government decided to hold provincial elections in 1937. Dr. B.R. Ambedkar set up the "Independent Labor Party" in August 1936 to contest the elections in the Bombay province. He and many candidates of his party were elected to the Bombay Legislative Assembly.

In 1937, Dr. Ambedkar introduced a Bill to abolish the "khoti" system of land tenure in the Konkan region, the serfdom of agricultural tenants and the Mahar "watan" system of working for the Government as slaves. A clause of an agrarian bill referred to the depressed classes as "Harijans," or people of God. Bhimrao strongly opposed this title for the untouchables. He argued that if the "untouchables" were people of God then all others would be people of monsters. He was against any such reference. But the

Indian National Congress succeeded in introducing the term Harijan. Ambedkar felt bitter that they could not have any say in what they were called.

Ambedkar's educational philosophy was greatly influenced by Prof. John Dewey of Columbia University who was a philosopher of nationalism and pragmation and wrote prolifically on the American educational system and culture. Ambedkar considered education as a prerequisite for any kind of organization and movement of oppressed classes. That is why his advice "Educate, organize and agitate". He firmly believed that education could bring not only new consciousness among backward communities but also impel them towards praxis of self-liberation. Later he made constitutional provision for free and compulsory education to all. His preference for education rather than material gain is evident from his speech on the Bombay University Act Amendment Bill in Bombay Legislative Council on 5th October 1927. Ambedkar said, "We may forgo material benefits of civilization, but we cannot forgo our right and opportunity to reap the benefits of the highest education to the fullest extent." His emphasis was on higher education. He said, "Coming as I do from the lowest order of Hindu society. . . . Nothing can achieve this purpose except the spread of higher education. This is in my opinion the panacea of our social troubles." (Dhaktode 71)

In 1947, when India became independent, the first Prime Minister Pt. Jawaharlal Nehru, invited Dr. Bhimrao Ambedkar, who had been elected as a Member of the Constituent Assembly from Bengal, to join his Cabinet as a Law Minister. The Constituent Assembly entrusted the job of drafting the Constitution to a committee and Dr. Ambedkar was elected as Chairman of this Drafting Committee. In February 1948, Dr. Ambedkar presented the Draft Constitution before the people of India; it was adopted on November 26, 1949.

In October 1948, Dr. Ambedkar submitted the Hindu Code Bill to the Constituent Assembly in an attempt to codify the Hindu law. The Bill caused great divisions even in the Congress party. Consideration for the bill was postponed to September 1951. When the Bill was taken up it was truncated. A dejected Ambedkar relinquished his position as Law Minister.

On May 24, 1956, on the occasion of Buddha Jayanti, Ambedkar declared in Bombay, that he would adopt Buddhism in October. On 0ctober 14, 1956 he embraced Buddhism along with many of his followers. On December 6, 1956, Baba Saheb Dr. B.R. Ambedkar died in his sleep. For his yeoman service to the nation, B.R. Ambedkar was bestowed with Bharat Ratna in 1990.

Just as the problems of the depressed classes attracted Ambedkar's attention, the problems of women too were a priority task for him and he sincerely did work for their emancipation. He raised his powerful voice to support the cause of women through his speeches that he delivered on various forums in various capacities and through his writings. As the Law and the Labour member of the Viceroy's Executive Council, as the chairman of the Drafting Committee of the Constituent Assembly of India and as the Union Minister for Law in the union council of ministers in independent India, he was mainly instrumental in drafting various bills like the Hindu Code Bill and in persistently striving to enact it into a law, for he always believed that it would revolutionize women's socio-economic conditions. (Mudbi 239) He carefully studied and analyzed Indian society. He strongly felt that there was a need for social reform and reorganization of Indian society on the basis of equality, freedom and fraternity. He believed that such a social reform would be possible only through education of the masses.

Dr. Ambedkar's questions, doubts, clarifications for women's emancipation can be seen in his works like *The Rise and Fall of Hindu Women* and in his unpublished writings like *Revolution and Counter Revolution in Ancient India: Women and the Counter Revolution*. Moreover, Dr. Ambedkar had touched upon the subject of women's status in his work *Caste in India* and *Annihilation of Caste* and also in his work entitled Riddles *in Hinduism*.

Ambedkar's detailed study and analysis of the history of the rise and the fall in the status of Hindu women is thought-provoking, serving as a useful guide for future reformers.

Ambedkar's whole study and analysis of the problem of Indian women centers on his perspective of the creation of patriarchy in all the religious and social institutions and his reasoned contempt for Manu and *Manusmriti*. He sought to change the laws of Manu which were misogynist and reduced a woman to a commodity. This whole historical exercise that he made was not a mere academic exercise. He made this exercise more as a response to the slavish condition of woman. He went into the historical origin to correctly formulate the problem and find solutions. This attempt of Ambedkar is rooted in his understanding of the problem in its historical context and a humanistic democratic perspective.

Ambedkar offers new insights into the progress by which patriarchy becomes established and institutionalized in the Indian context. He also notes that the emerging of cruel practices like child marriage, ban on widow remarriage, harsh rules of the widowhood and *sati,* occurred during Manu Shastra era.

Ambedkar thought that until and unless he studies the Hindu texts he cannot argue with the orthodox people. He was also interested in knowing what had brought about such inequality in the Hindu society. For this he had to learn Sanskrit, as the texts were written in Sanskrit. He did not get an opportunity to learn this in India because at that time the people of the low caste were not permitted to read and listen to Sanskrit and Ambedkar belonged to those lower castes. But his interest did not allow this to deter him and he learnt it from a German scholar. After deeply analyzing the texts he wrote on many topics quoting from the Sanskrit text itself and arguing about the inhuman practices of inequality which were Carried out in the name of religion which led to the exploitation of the weaker section of society. He criticized Manu the Hindu law giver for perpetrating his unequal laws into society.

What Ambedkar said or did had the limitation of historical possibilities; he would not say anything for the sake of postulating. He craved for change and strove to bring it about with a pragmatic approach. In the context of his championship of women, his approach needs to be understood from this perspective.

Ambedkar clearly pointed out that women enjoyed equality before the pre-Buddhist Brahmanism. It was only when Manu formulated his laws that unequal practices like child marriage, *sati* were newly introduced. He pointed out: "The rule of Manu that a girl should be married before she had reached puberty is a new rule. In pre-Buddhist Brahmanism marriages were performed not only after puberty but they were performed when girls had reached an age when they could be grown up." (BAWS, Vol. 3, 294)

He further said there was sufficient evidence to prove whatever he said. He said the same about *sati*: "In the pre-Buddhist Brahmanism there was no prohibition on widow remarriage. The fact that the Sanskrit language contains words such as *Punarbhu* (woman who has undergone a second marriage ceremony) and *Punarbharan* (second husband) show that such marriages were quite common under the pre-Buddhist Brahmanism." (*Ibid.*)

So Ambedkar raised the question such as: "Why were these changes made by the triumphant Brahmanism? What did Brahmanism want to achieve by having girls married before they had become pubert by denying the widow the right to marry again and by telling her to put herself to death by immolating herself in the funeral pyre of her deceased husband?" (BAWS 3, 295)

Writing about evil customs such as *sati,* enforced widowhood and child marriage, Dr. Ambedkar says, "Like fossils they tell their own History. Though many have sung in praise of these customs, nothing can tell us the causes of their origin and existence: philosophies grew around them to justify and some philosophies that created castes were sweetened to gild the pill." (BAWS 1. 5)

Ambedkar as a historian wrote in his book 'Who were the Shudras': "An history ought to be exact, sincere and impartial;

free from passion, unbiased by interest, fear, resentment or affection; and faithful to the truth, which is the mother of history . . . a readiness to examine all evidence even though it be spurious." (BAWS 7, opening page)

Looking into the justification of C.V. Vaidya who offered an explanation for child marriage (History of India, II) that child marriage was introduced to prevent girls from joining the Buddhist order of nuns. Ambedkar was not satisfied with the answer. He further raised the question: "The question is not why girl marriage was introduced. The question is why Manu allowed so much discrepancy in the ages of the bride and bridegroom." (BAWS 3, 295)

Ambedkar was aware of the arguments of some historians like Mr. Kane who wrote about *sati* in 'History of Dharmasastra' that *sati* was not something new; it also existed in India in ancient times as it did in other parts of the world. Ambedkar was not convinced by such explanation of the historians and said, "Mr. Kane's explanation that the prevalence of sati by reference to laws of inheritance does not appear to me very convincing. It may be because under the Hindu Law of inheritance as it prevailed in Bengal . . . why sati was practiced on such a large scale in Bengal. But it does not explain how it arose nor how it came to be practiced in other parts of India." (BAWS 3, 295)

He further said with regard to prohibition of widow remarriage, there was no explanation whatsoever. He raised questions about why a woman was prohibited from marrying, why she was required to lead a life of misery and why she was disfigured. After a thorough analysis of the cause of downfall of women he said, "My explanation for girl marriage, enforced widowhood and sati is quite different and I offer it for what it is worth." (BAWS 3, 296) Ambedkar related the downfall of women to the caste system. To maintain the purity of caste women were targeted. He put his explanation thus: "Thus the superposition of endogamy over exogamy meant the creation of caste. But this is not an easy affair. Let us take an imaginary group. . . . It is absolutely necessary to circumscribe a circle without which people should not contract marriage." (BAWS 3, 296)

He explained that in normal groups the two sexes were more or less evenly distributed, and generally speaking there is equality between those of the same age. Further he said; just to maintain caste among all, this type of injustice was created towards women because of her not being as aggressive as men. So Ambedkar said, "The problem of caste then ultimately resolved itself into one of repairing the disparity between the marriageable units of the two sexes within . . . she can be disposed of in two different ways so as to preserve the endogamy of the caste." (BAWS 3, 226-27)

Ambedkar interpreted this as a way to overcome the problem of free women who must be disposed, or else through intermarriage they would violate the endogamy of the group. So these inhuman rules or laws were made against women to control them. But this rule was not the same for men. Ambedkar said, "The problem of surplus man (-widower) is much more important and much more difficult than that of the surplus woman in a group that desires to make itself into a caste." (BAWS 3, 297)

Ambedkar further analyzed this issue: "He is a dominant figure in every group and of the two sexes has greater prestige. With this traditional superiority of man over woman his wishes have always been consulted. Woman on the other hand have been an easy prey to all kinds of iniquitous injunctions, religious, social or economic. But man as a maker of injunctions is most often above them all. Such being the case you cannot accord the same kind of treatment to a surplus man as you can to a surplus woman in a caste." (BAWS 3, 297-98) Ambedkar continued by saying: "This, in my opinion, is the general mechanism of a caste in a system of castes . . . if this is true, our task will be amply rewarded if we scrutinize the solution the Hindus arrived at, to meet the problems of the surplus man and surplus woman." (BAWS 3, 299)

And in connection with the questions he raised on why woman is targeted, he says, "Regarding the question as to why they arose,

I submit that they were needed to create the structure of caste and the philosophies in honour of them were indented to popularize . . . but it does not deprive it of its real nature, that of a means." (BAWS 3, 300-1)

To clarify it using metaphoric expression, he said, "You may pass a law that all cats are dogs, just as you can call a means an end. But you can no more change the nature of means thereby than you can turn cats into dogs; consequently I am justified in holding that, regard them as ends or as means. Sati, widowhood and girl marriage are customs that were primarily intended to solve the problem of the surplus man and surplus woman in a caste and to maintain its endogamy. Strict endogamy could not be preserved without these customs, while caste without endogamy is fake." (BAWS 3, 301)

Concluding his view over sati, child marriage and widowhood Ambedkar said, "This is my explanation of these new rules, made by Brahmanism. That explanation of these new rules, made by Brahmanism may not be acceptable to all. But there can be no doubt that Brahmanism was taking all means possible to prevent inter marriages between the different classes taking place." (BAWS 3, 301)

In his *Annihilation of Caste*, Ambedkar advocated inter-caste marriage as one of the solutions to the problem. But he stresses that the belief in the shastras is the root cause of maintaining castes. He therefore suggested: "Make every man and woman free from the thralldom of the 'Shastras'. Cleanse their mind of the pernicious notions founded on the 'Shastras' and he or she will interdine and intermarry." (BAWS 1, xiv-xv)

Ambedkar said that Manu can hardly be said to be more considerate to women than he was to the shudras. He starts with a low opinion of women. We can see the quotes of Manu on this in Ambedkar's writings and speeches in Vol. 3, on pages 313 to 317. Ambedkar said that the laws of Manu against women are of a piece with this view. Women are not to be free under any circumstances.

Ambedkar further stressed, "The principle of graded inequality runs through the whole of the Manu Smriti. There is no department of life in which he has not introduced his principle of graded inequality. For a complete and thorough exposition of it, . . . how in the hands of Manu the principle of graded inequality became embedded in social life." (BAWS 3, 317)

Ambedkar expressed his disagreement in an exclamation: "This the Hindus regard as a very lofty ideal for a woman!!! (BAWS 3, 316) He very authoritatively said further, "The severity of these laws against shudras and women show that the phenomenal rise of these classes during the Buddhist regime had not only offended the Brahmins but had become intolerable to them . . . and pursuit of happiness [due to which] India became a decaying if not a dead nation." (BAWS 3, 316-17)

We can see his erudite scholarship in analyzing the issue of inequality of women in society in his writings "The Women and the Counter-Revolution". In this he discusses all the points made by Manu with regard to women. He argues using as his basis the position of women in pre-Manu's time when she rose to the highest penance of learning and education. So, according to him it was Manu who was the cause of the downfall of women in India. Ambedkar was so persuasive in his arguments that he brought out many examples of women occupying high positions and the respect they got before Manu's laws. He wrote, "That women in pre-Manu days were highly respected cannot be disputed. Among the Ratnis who played so prominent part in the coronation of the king in Ancient India was the queen and the king made her an offering as he did to the others. Not only did the king elect to pay homage to the queen, he worshipped his other wives of lower castes." (BAWS Vol. 3, 432-33).

He stressed his point by quoting Kautilya's days as well. There was no ban on women or widow remarriage. Women had the right to enjoy their property. Unlike Manu every precaution was taken to guarantee economic independence to a woman. He further said, "Surprising as it may appear in Kautilya's time, a wife could bring an action in a court of law against her husband for assault and defamation." (BAWS 3, 437) So Ambedkar raised a question: when women were free and equal partners of men, why did Manu degrade them? His arguments were so powerful that even today their importance is felt in every field.

Ambedkar's assumption was that there was a relation between the steep rise of the caste system and the steady decline of the position and the status of women in India. Ambedkar further contended that the *Manusmriti*, the epitome of brahmanism, was a counter revolution on the assumption that Buddhism was a revolution radically altering the status of women. But historically speaking, the decline of the status of women was only a continuous process begun during the *Vedic* age and carried to its logical end by the *Manusmriti*. Once again, if it is conceded that patriarchy emerged before *Manusmriti,* then the latter could not be the cause of women's downfall and, therefore, was not a 'counter revolution', but a continuation. However, it was the rigidity of the patriarchy which was made as a rule in the form of law, which Ambedkar was talking about.

Dr. Ambedkar's contribution to female emancipation can profusely be seen in all his works and speeches where he explicitly draws out the links between the subordination of women and the caste system. His arguments are based on the following aspects: Women are the gateways to the caste system, the caste system consolidates further the subordination of women. Brahminical culture is responsible for the subordination of women. Ambedkar suggested that to counter this system he has to do something. So he brought the Hindu Code Bill as a counter to caste based patriarchal law, encouraged untouchable women to have a specific identity and become a political force, and insisted that violent practices against women must be opposed.

While analyzing the caste system in the essay *Caste in India*, Vol. I, he refers to castes as enclosed classes which is the origin of untouchability, being located in beef eating, and concludes that "the absence of inter-marriage or endogamy is the one characteristic that can be called the essence of castes". He painstakingly underlined the intrinsic relations between the caste system and the subordination of women.

The restriction of marriage to the caste group presents some problems. Normally the sex ratio in any given group is likely to be balanced, that is, men and women tend to be present in equal number. A severe imbalance in this ratio is likely to create problems in the form of 'surplus men' or 'surplus women'. That is, if a wife dies before her husband the man is rendered 'surplus' and vice versa. The group then faces a problem of how this surplus man/woman was going to be disposed of. According to Dr. Ambedkar, in order to maintain the sex ratio and perpetuate endogamy and thereby the caste system, four practices were employed, i.e., the practice of *sati,* enforced widowhood, enforced celibacy, the marriage of child brides with older men or widowers.

Dr. Ambedkar proceeds to analyze each of these practices and establishes how they ensure the balance in the sex ratio and makes the emergence of caste groups possible. We can see his scholarly presentations of such difficult topics and his authority over the subject as a decisive factor in the ensuring emancipation of Indian women, especially of the so-called lower castes.

Ambedkar's support of the women's cause was a life-long engagement. For instance, with regard to inter caste marriages Dr. Ambedkar's observations are valuable. Inter-caste marriages have always been opposed by the caste system: custom, religion and law alike have banned this practice. Dr. Ambedkar in his work *Philosophy of Hindustan* discussed the issue in great detail. Quoting from the *Manusmriti,* he argues that many had strict rules saying that an upper caste man could first marry a woman from his own caste; in his subsequent marriages, he could marry women from the lower *varnas*. However, a *shudra* woman could marry only a *shudra* man. Thus Manu's opposition to inter-caste marriage is apparent and it becomes mandatory to marry a woman from one's own varna. Despite these severe regulations, if inter-caste marriages do take place, then the law that regulates it is patriarchal and biased.

As noted earlier Ambedkar's assumption that the atrocious evils like female child marriages, ban on widow remarriages, widowhood and sati were the result of the endogamous nature of the caste system, requiring male-female parity within the caste group, was also questionable; while on one hand, women practiced widowhood and even *sati*, on the other hand, men continued the practice of polygamy and were also allowed exogamy. This appeared to him as a crucial issue requiring immediate change. He warns against the results of these means by saying, "Idealization of means is necessary . . . perhaps motivated to endow them with greater efficacy calling a means an end does not harm, except that it disguises its real character." (BAWS 1, 14)

This shows how the real situation disproves the assumption that widowhood and *sati* arose out of the need for maintaining male-female parity within a caste group. This was not to deny that under the endogamous caste system permitted by notions of purity and pollution, women as procreators had an extra premium attached to the purity of their sexuality which went beyond ordinary 'patriarchy'. Still, the institutions of widowhood and *sati* were inexplicable within these formulas.

Ambedkar repeatedly reiterated that it was the endogamous nature of the caste system that led to the subordination and degradation of women. But this feature of men controlling women, their sexuality, pro-creativity and labour, known as patriarchy, still prevails even in societies where there is no caste.

It is acknowledged that women's subordination is always linked with the emergence of class division in society. The first-class antagonism which appears in history coincided with the development of the antagonism between man and woman in monogamous marriages and the first-class oppression with that of the female sex by the male. Therefore, it is no surprise that the misfortune of Indian women became linked with the rise of the early caste system which corresponds to the progressive development of class society. Indeed, the contours of the changing status of Indian women through history are but an echo of the more or less similar worldwide process. Ambedkar explained that women were the center point in the caste system and so they were targeted by being deprived of rights like education, economic independence; but they had no voice to speak for themselves. But because of the reform movements they started coming out of their ignorance and started thinking about themselves. At this time of their awakening the clear arguments of Ambedkar helped them to become aware of their subordination in society.

Ambedkar suggested that endogamous unions with their parameters of purity had to be rethought. Otherwise, exogamy could not be avoided. The upper castes did not want this because it would end the caste system and with it the advantages that accrued to the Brahmins. Ambedkar bolsters his arguments by citing new laws prohibiting varna inter-marriages. He particularly draws the attention to the prohibition of high caste women from marrying low caste men. But there was no logic behind the fact that a high caste man had access to a woman of low caste with no responsibility towards the offspring. This was made possible by the new rule of matriliny (*Matrusavarna*) to be followed in case of high caste men marrying low caste women (*Anuloma* marriage). This, in effect, was the privilege of males of higher caste, to lawfully commit prostitution with low caste women and they were absolved of any further responsibility. (Mudbi 241)

Though a few scholars had attempted to sketch the history of women in India, who had examined the changes that had occurred over a period of time and discussed the difficulties that Indian women faced since the *Vedic* period, yet none suggested any remedial measures to curb the pernicious tendencies of the caste system. This is the fundamental and innovative argument advanced by Ambedkar.

Ambedkar on 25 December 1927 burned *Manusmriti*. This is also a form of protest discourse to show his protest against the injustice done in the society. He thundered that his aim was not only to remove inequality but to destroy chaturvarna, as the root cause lies there. According to him the root of untouchability and subordination of women was in prohibition of inter-caste marriages that he decided to break. He appealed to higher varnas to let this "Social Revolution" take place peacefully, to discard the sastras, and accept the principle of justice.

There was a strong reaction in the Brahmanical press; Ambedkar was called "Bheemaasura" by one newspaper. Dr. Ambedkar justified the burning of *Manusmriti* in various articles. He ridiculed those people by saying that they have not read the *Manusmriti,* and declared that he would never accept it. Further he said for those who say it is an outdated booklet so why give importance to it, he invited attention to atrocities on dalits and women and said these are because Hindus were still following this book. And he further asked, if it is outdated, how does it matter to the opponents if somebody burns it. For those who enquire, what is achieved by Ambedkar burning it, he retorted, what did M. Gandhi achieved by burning foreign clothes, what was achieved by those who burned Miss Mayo's book "Mother India" in New York, what was achieved by boycotting Simon Commission formed to frame political reforms? These were the forms of registering the protests, so was ours against *Manusmriti*.

Buddhism offered an alternate scheme to some extent, but being made weak and ineffective on the whole, only served to prompt brahminism to rectify its loopholes and clamp down the already rigid norms of the caste system and the rules of degraded womanhood under the guise of secular and religious codes.

His western education taught him to have immense faith in democratic values. He openly declared that "Freedom, Equality and Fraternity," the triumvirate, would be his philosophy. He did not accept these principles from the French Revolution, but from Buddhism. He stated that freedom and equality could be protected only if there was a feeling of brotherhood among the people. Another name of brotherhood is humanity, and humanity is the true religion. (17, 503) Dr. Ambedkar's interest in political ideology was as varied as his intellectual abilities. Besides western philosophy and science, he developed a deep interest in socialism.

Ambedkar wrote a rejoinder to an article published in 'Eve's Weekly' on 21, 1950, under the title "Our New Republic" where it stated that Indian women were used to statecraft long before they ever did in Europe. The Ramayana and Mahabharata were full of instances of such women. Ambedkar questioned the author that was he hinting at the fact: "Draupadi, the chief female character of the Mahabharata was gambled away by her husband or husbands (because she had five) or that Sita, who had heroically rejected all advances of her captor Ravana, was rewarded with distrust and doubts in her purity, put to the fire-ordeal and banished into the jungle?" (BAWS 17, part 2, 495)

Ambedkar clarified his point to the author by saying, "If the position of women in those days had been what the writer of the above-mentioned article would have us believe, then we wonder why Draupadi had never been given a chance to gamble away her five husbands, or Sita an opportunity to send her calumniators and doubters on the pyre or into the woods?" (BAWS 17, part 2, 495) He further wrote: "It certainly would have been more correct in this connection to say that the Women of India in those times were used by statecraft." (BAWS 17, part 2, 495)

The article also said that Indian women enjoyed statecraft long before the women of European for which Ambedkar said: "As to the women of Europe, I cannot say whether they were lagging behind their sisters in India in this respect, but I am quite sure that when some of them got an opportunity to meddle with statecraft they were quick to make use of it." (BAWS 17, part 2, 495)

To justify his point he showed the comparison of the European women and Indian women and said, "If Queen Elizabeth had been in the place of Draupadi she would probably have executed her five husbands as she executed her unfortunate lover Lord Essex. But in my opinion Draupadi without statecraft was a more lovable woman than Queen Bessie with all her political power and cunning." (BAWS 17, part 2, 495)

Likewise he gave many more examples of European women who reached to the supreme power from the lowest position like Empress Maria Theresa of Austria, or Empress Theodora of Byzantium. He asserted, "I do not think this would be the ideal of Indian womanhood, just as I do not think that statecraft adds one inch to the dignity of a woman." (BAWS 17, part 2, 496)

He further mentioned: "Even if it were true that in India women were used to statecraft, long before they ever did in Europe out author apparently was not able to find any historically verified instances of an early period than the Rani of Jhansi and Chandbibi, who both belong to the most recent epochs of India's history." (BAWS 17, part 2, 496)

But for Ambedkar what was more bothersome was the astonishing statement of the article that Buddhist theory seems to have first thrust women into the background. He asserted that he had scrutinized the Buddhist sacred text and their teachings, and he had found no special theory about women, but only about the human species in general. He said, "All through Buddhist history it was a special feature of Buddhist Society that women had a far favourable position than in most Non-Buddhist countries. The fundamental equality of man and woman has been the lodestar of Buddhist Society from its earliest beginnings." (BAWS 17, part 2, 496)

He further clarified the position of women in Buddhist countries and said, "Anybody who has lived in Buddhist countries, be in Ceylon, Burma, Siam, Indo-China, Tibet, knows that the status of women is astonishingly high. Because the Buddhist wife does not look up to her husband as to a god, she is not expected to eat after her husband has finished his meal, or to immolate herself after her husband's death as an alternative to a life of utter dejection and privation. On the contrary, she is free to leave her husband if she feels that she cannot live with him, and she does not become a social outcast after her husband's death, but can remarry if she desires so." (BAWS 17, part 2, 496) He also said, "Women may have their own affairs, in fact in Burma as well as in Tibet (of the countries I can speak of my own experience) women are perfect equals of men, socially as well as in respect of business affairs, and they often show more enterprise and ability than men, who gladly leave these things to their womenfolk." (*Ibid.*)

Ambedkar gave this explanation because the author of the article in Eve's Weekly criticized that Buddha had a prejudice against women and was forever exhorting men to beware of them. Ambedkar according to him Buddha was the most broadminded, most liberal and tolerant of all the great teachers of the past.

Ambedkar expressed his views on religion while discussing the position of women in society. As with all his writings, here too he goes to the root of the matter. In a reply to the charge made against the Buddha and the cause for the *Mahaparinibhana Sutta* which, he states, is a later interpolation because the '*Sutta Pitaka*' was written by monks for monks 400 years after the death of the Buddha. Further, he holds that the very fact that women of all classes met Buddha for religious instructions makes it clear that he did not shun women. He maintains that though the Buddha was dreadfully keen on maintaining celibacy, he did not shun, nor did he advise the Bhikkhus to shun all contact with women as their mothers, sisters or daughters. Ambedkar cites the analogy of nunneries working in subordination to monasteries in justification of the Bhikkuni Sanghas being subordinated to the Bhikkhu Sanghas and justifies Buddha's forming two separate Sanghas: "The Buddha knew what a great force sex instinct is with life of both man as well a woman. To use the Buddha's own words it is this instinct which drives a man in woman's bondage and a woman in man's bondage. This force, if given an opportunity to have its force, the rule of celibacy could not last for a minute. To have the rule of celibacy he had to organize two separate Sanghas." (*Bheem Patrika* 12-13)

Dr. Ambedkar hypothesizes that the decline in the status and the position of Indian women occurred due to many reasons. The rigidity of the caste system was the first and the foremost reason. As Buddhism, free from the rigidity of caste, offered more opportunities for liberty and equality to all including women, a large number of people who felt deprived or stifled under Vedic religion eventually turned their backs on it to follow Buddhism, especially women and shudras.

Ambedkar was always in search of equality and he found that in Buddhism there was equality of all human beings which included mankind. Talking about Buddha's four Noble Truths, Ambedkar said, "The second Truth is, the cause of misery is evil. It is the worst thing in a degraded society. To overcome this social malady, the Religion of 'Reason' is necessary as it is based on 'non-violence' and 'Peace'. For this the man has to cultivate the power within him to grow into Buddha." (Damodar 100)

Ambedkar further quoted Buddha who had said: "Believe not because you have been made to believe from childhood, but reason it all out and after you have analyzed it, then if you find that it will do good to one and all, believe it, live up to it and help others to live up to it." (Damodar 111) Ambedkar said reason enables man to arrange and systematize knowledge so as to construct truth. So talking about conversion he declared, 'Religion is for man and not man for religion'. (Damodar 111) On the eve of his conversion to Buddhism, he said, "There was only one man who raised his voice against the separatism and untouchability, and that was Lord Buddha." (Damodar 98)

Ambedkar reiterated the importance of life in society based on religious principles. This means, in turn, a social responsibility in the absence of which, there is imbalance in the society. In this context he said, "one of the greatest things I find in Buddhism is that its system is a democratic system." (Damodar 111)

His thoughts on Buddhism helped him draft the constitution of India on the bases of the principles of a democratic system. His definition of democracy is that it is "a form and method of government whereby revolutionary changes in the economic and social life are brought about without bloodshed." (Damodar 112)

For Ambedkar conversion was essential because he knew religion was very important for man, so he wanted a religion where equality prevailed. This was also done keeping in view women because the eight-fold path of Buddhism taught people to be away from speaking lies, not to drink alcohol, not to gamble, etc. Most of the men indulged in these, due to which the condition of women deteriorated. To bring a change in the condition of women Ambedkar adopted this religion. Above all he wanted to embrace Buddhism because this religion was from our own land, i.e., India.

Apart from his academic writings, when Ambedkar became a leader in public life, women were the major force in all his struggles. Women's issues were also the main planks in his fortnightly *Mooknayak* and *Bahishkrit Bharat*. Dr. Ambedkar stressed on education as necessary for females as there would be much progress. Dalit women responded very positively to Dr. Ambedkar's advice. But the elite women from the upper caste did not accept the progressive policies of Ambedkar because, in spite of their progress, they were under the pressure of tradition "Dalit feminism" has drawn copiously from this pool. However, feminist discourse at large has remained ignorant of the rich and complex interpretations of caste and gender as conceptualized by the architect of the Constitution; there is urgency for feminist discourse to turn to Ambedkar. A category of women undifferentiated by caste does not exist for feminists to mobilize. Now the pressure is not to talk about gender in isolation, but to include class, caste and other factors. Therefore, there is a need to reclaim Dr. Ambedkar's writings as feminist classics.

Much before the Indian feminist discourse of caste and gender interlinked, Dr. Ambedkar talked about issues of women and in fact he had expressed more on women than on the issue of untouchability itself. He argues that the question of annihilating untouchability is more an issue for women than for men. While addressing the untouchable women at the Mahad Satyagraha Parishad, Speech published in (Bahishkrit Bharat, 1928) he said: "You gave birth to us men and other people treat us even worse than they would treat animals . . . at places even our shadows are not allowed. Others acquire positions of prestige in offices and government but we, born to you, are not even the least prestigious jobs. For, we are considered to be lowly status. . . . How are we in any way different from the children of the Kayastha and other Severna women sitting in this sabha? . . . and yet why is it that their progeny is acceptable to all but those born to you are so insulted that they are denied even the basic right to be human? Have you even given this a thought? Why is birth from your wombs considered a sin?" (Pardeshi 1998, 42)

He was a person who believed in the importance of the home. He understood that the house centers around the mother. If a mother can have a hold on the family, every house, the smallest unit in the society, will be the core of a revolution. In fact, he went, sat and talked with the under-privileged and down-trodden in their battered houses. We can see the polemical style of Ambedkar. He was very clear and in a more understanding way, he built confidence in the poor and deprived women. He encouraged them to question themselves and act upon the discrimination imposed on them. Establishing the relationship between the caste system and the subordination of women, Ambedkar argues that the caste system being a hierarchical one, due to the lower the position of the women in the hierarchy, her exploitation is more intense. In this context, he calls upon women to join the struggle for the annihilation of the caste system. In Ambedkar's view, to break the power structure of the caste system the need was women's participation in the movement. He wanted them to develop reasoning and question the atrocities levied on them.

The discourse of Rammohun Roy was mainly to men of his time, because women were not aware of their progress at that time. Now slowly with the awakening emancipation process women got the opportunity to get education and they too slowly started coming out of their homes in the public life and so for Gandhi and Ambedkar the audience were both men and women. The participation of men and women were equal and so there was a change in their articulation. More confidence building speeches can be seen when they address women. Because the need of women to get exposure to public life was the need of the hour.

At the Mahad Satyagraha Parishad, which was Ambedkar's first movement to fight against injustice, many depressed class women also participated in the Satyagraha. In his speech, he repeatedly underlined the importance of education to women. He addressed the gathering saying: "You must also educate your daughters. Knowledge and education are not for men alone. These are important for women too. If you want your next generation to progress, then you must educate your daughters. If a woman is educated, the whole family is put in touch with knowledge and education and the reform in ideas and ideologies become possible." (Pardeshi 1998, 42)

In his speech addressing the All-India Depressed Classes Women's Conference, on July 20, 1942, he said: "I am very happy to have this occasion to address you. There cannot be an occasion of great happiness to anyone interested in the advancement of the Depressed Classes than to witness this gathering of women. That you would assemble in such vast numbers—almost 20,000 to 25,000 strong . . . would have been unthinkable 10 years ago. I am a great believer in women's organization." (BAWS 17, part 3, 282)

Ambedkar developed self-respect and confidence in the women of low castes and said with confidence that they can change the age-old custom of their being inferior. As suggested by him they started to think over the questions he raised and started sending their children to schools, started keeping their houses clean and above all started raising their voice against the inequality against them. Expressing his faith in the capability of women, he said, "I know what they can do to improve the condition of the society if they are convinced. In the eradication of social evils they have rendered great services. I will testify to that from my own experience. Ever since I began to work among the Depressed Classes, I made a point to carry women along with me. That is why you will see that our Conferences are always mixed Conferences. I measure the progress which women have achieved, and when I see this assembly, I feel both convinced and happy that we have progressed." (BAWS 17, part 3, 282)

As a guide to all the women of the depressed class he advised them to improve their living conditions because keeping themselves neat and clean, giving education to their children and teaching their children to develop confidence and improve their lives will help them to change their living standards. All the women took his advice seriously because they learnt that whatever he said was true. They found him as their messiah who was struggling to improve their lives and also raise them in statues society. "I shall tell you a few things which I think you should bear in mind. Learn to be clean; keep free from all vices. Give education to your children. Instill ambition in them. Inculcate in their minds that they are destined to be great. Remove from them all inferiority complexes. Don't be in a hurry to marry: marriage is a liability. You should not impose it on your children unless financially they are able to meet the liabilities arising from marriage. Those who will marry will bear in mind that to have too many children is a crime. That parental duty lies in giving each child a better start than its parents had." (BAWS 17, part 3, 282-283)

Ambedkar expressed these views on marriage to the women at the meeting. His view was that, since their children are economically independent they should not think of marriage at all. He also said that producing many children was not the duty of the parents but to give them a good and respectable living was more important. Like a father, he advised them on every topic to make their home a happy home. The most important advice he gave to women was to be on an equal footing with their husband and not subordinate to him or a slave. "Above all, let each girl who marries stand up to her husband, claim to her husband as equal, and refuse to be a slave. I am sure if you follow this advice you will bring honor and glory to yourself and to Depressed Classes." (BAWS 17, part 3, 283)

The above speech reflects his understanding of the basic problems of the women of depressed classes; keeping themselves clean, educating the children, and inculcating in their minds that they are destined to be great, not to be in a hurry to marry, being a friend to their husbands and not slaves—all this shows how much concern he had for their cause. We can see the softness in his address to the poor people, compared to the erudite and strong writings in English. He built confidence in them for their progress.

This speech can be looked into as confidence-building even today to the depressed class because unless a person develops confidence in himself it is not possible for his progress. Ambedkar's advice was imbibed by the women word by word and they strove for their progress which was kept away from them for many years in the name of religion. With this confidence, the Dalit women were able to participate in all fields along with other women for their progress.

Ambedkar's opposition to the atrocities on women is also apparent in the speech that he delivered at a gathering of prostitutes. Ambedkar coming from a poor background knew the suffering of the poor and this type of advice is relevant from him to improve the condition of women. He emphasized that this method of making money for their living was wrong. He advices them that poverty was not something new to them so they have to face it but getting defeated in the name of prostitution was not advisable. At the gathering of *devadasis, vaghaya* and *murali* in 1938, he said, "Stop practising prostitution. Poverty is not something we should fear. It has been with us ever since our birth. So do not practice this occupation for fear of poverty." (BAWS 17, Part 3, 150)

Ambedkar at a meeting at Damodar Thackersey Hall, Bombay, on 16 July 1936, spoke to men and women belonging to the Devadasi, Potraje, Bhute, Aradhi and Jogtini sects. The meeting was held to accord support to the mass conversion move especially to the women, most of whom had come from Kamathipura. He addressed, "whether you change your religion along with us or not, it does not matter much to me. But I insist if you want to be with the rest of us you must give up your disgraceful life. The Mahar women of Kamathipura are a shame to the community . . . you will ask me how you are to make your living. I am not going to tell you. There are hundreds of ways of doing it." ((BAWS 17, part 3, 150)

Poverty which drove women to sell their bodies was perceived by him as an atrocity against women. This was seen in his act of severely opposing prostitution. Keeping to this principle, he refused to accept money donated by Pattahe Babu Rao, a Brahmin *tamasha* artist, arguing that the money was got from making Pavala Bai, an untouchable woman, dance on the *tamasha* floor. It is untouchable women who are most exploited by caste-based prostitution such as the practices of *devadasis*, and this was strongly condemned by Dr. Ambedkar. He sent a message to them that in the name of poverty they cannot do wrong in society, which would not only be harmful to themselves but to the society as a whole.

Ambedkar had such unshakeable faith in women that he repeatedly said that until women should be involved in every field otherwise there will be no progress in our country. He exhorted women to active public life by giving a slogan on education, unity and agitation when he said, "Unity is meaningless without the accomplishment of women. Education is fruitless without educated women. Agitation is incomplete without the strength of women". (Dandavate 32) As part of his movement to emancipate the depressed classes and women he started colleges for them in Bombay and Aurangabad. He took special interest in these colleges in spite of his busy schedule.

Ambedkar drafted several documents which were to shape the constitutional development in India. He remained a votary of constitutional democracy throughout. He also felt that certain core principles needed to inform not merely the institutional complex of governance but society at large.

He worked against the discrimination against women in the name of religion and law. Also now that women got the opportunity to get education and participate in public affairs their awareness grew and they expressed their feelings about their inequality. Ambedkar used a specialized discourse which combined his erudition and his empathy for women to formulate the Hindu Code Bill. He also bowed tenets from the laws of our country and other countries. In addition, he took in cognizance some issues raised by eminent thinkers both men and women. These he presented to the Parliament. Some of the issues he spoke about are Property Rights of women, abolition of caste restrictions in marriage, rights of women, divorce and adoption.

Ambedkar's aim in introducing the Hindu Code Bill was to codify the rules of Hindu Law which are scattered in innumerable decisions of the High Courts and of the Privy Council, which form a bewildering motley to the common man and give rise to constant litigation; therefore his work seeks to codify the law relating to different matters. Firstly it seeks to codify the law relating to the rights of property of a deceased Hindu who had died intestate without making a will, both female and male. Secondly, it prescribes a somewhat altered form of the order of succession among the different heirs to the property of a deceased dying intestate. Then it deals with the law of maintenance, marriage, divorce, adoption, minority and guardianship.

Ambedkar made a sizable contribution to women emancipation by making laws beneficial to them. While explaining his point over the Bill in the parliament he said that some general changes are made from the old Dayabhag rule and Mitakshara so far as female heirs are concerned. He said that the number of female heirs recognized now is much larger than under either the Mitakshara or the Dayabhag because there was a discrimination made among the female heirs, he said: "the Bill also seeks to make four changes in succession to a deceased Hindu, one change is that the widow, the daughter, the widow of a predeceased son, all are given the same rank as the son in the matter of inheritance. In addition to that, the daughter also is given a share in her father's property; her share is prescribed as half of that of the son." (Rodrigues 496)

Further being on the line of equality he clarified that as per the Hindu Law stridhan was given to a girl during her marriage. This would later go to her daughter. But Ambedkar made the change in the Bill as uniform rule of succession and said: "The second change which the Bill seeks to make with regard to the heirs is that the son also is now given a right to inherit the stridhan and he is given half the share which the daughter takes". (Rodrigues 497)

He made it clear that when a daughter gets half the share of the father's property, the son is also eligible to get half the share of the mother's property. The bill was to seek equality of position between the son and daughter. There was lot of opposition to the bill in the house of parliament because most of the members were from the upper caste and they were for the old Hindu laws where great discrimination was made against women. They did not favor change. Also as caste played a very dominating role the other reason was also that the members did not like a law made for them by a low caste man. Some women who were elected to the House also opposed the Bill because their awareness was very little and still they were under the tradition which had been dominating them since ages. It was very difficult for them to come suddenly out of that domination. So, to clarify their doubts Ambedkar spoke in the Parliament thus: "But it would be futile on my part to disguise the fact that there is a section—if not a large section, a section in the house—which feels a certain amount of compunction over certain parts of the Bill. Neither can I therefore think that it is only right, if you will permit me, to add a few general observations with regard to the points of controversy which I have noticed in several newspapers which I have been perusing ever since the Bill has been on the anvil." (Rodrigues 502) Ambedkar quoting some examples from the Hindu texts itself explains: "So far as the Bill is concerned, what it does is to arrive at a sort of compromise between the new and the old." (Rodrigues 502)

He said it was up to the people to adopt whichever system they wanted to follow. For instance those who follow the orthodox system, that is, marrying in their own caste or varna can do so. If some reformists who did not believe in Varna, caste or subcaste and marry of his choice, the law regards his marriage also as valid. But he feared: "Consequently, what will happen in Hindu society so far as marriage law is concerned is there will be a competition between the old and the new. And we hope those who are following the new path will win subsequently." (Rodrigues 503)

To make the point clear with the orthodox and the Vedhika he said, "There is no violation of a shastra, no violation of a smriti at all" (Rodrigues 503). Further while explaining the Hindu Code Bill because he stressed on uniformity and with regard to property rights he said, "I do not know how many members of this House are familiar with the intricacies of this subject. So far as I have been able to study this subject, I do not think that there is any subject in the Hindu Law which is so complicated, so intricate as the women's property" (Rodrigues 511).

Ambedkar knew from the arguments that most of them opposed women getting absolute property, because it was said that women are imbeciles, and they are subject to the influence of all sorts of people and so it would be very dangerous to leave women who may get influenced by all sorts of wily men and lose their property. Ambedkar questioned this type of argument and said, "In certain matters or certain kinds of property which is called stridhan property the Smritis are prepared to invest women with absolute rights. There can be no question at all that a woman has an absolute right over her stridhan property. She can dispose of it in any way she likes. My submission to the House is this. If the woman can be trusted to dispose of her stridhan property in the best way she likes, and nobody has ever raised an argument for the obliteration of that rule of Mitakshara, the burden of proof lies upon the opponents who say that the other part of the property, namely, the widow's estate, which the woman has inherited, should not become her absolute property." (Rodrigues 512-13)

Talking about woman's share in the property Ambedkar said, "There are many people in this world, in India today both orthodox and unorthodox who cannot help producing daughters; They do. I do not know what would happen to this world if daughters were not born . . . they do not extend the same love and affection which a parent is bound to extend both to the male and female issue." (Rodrigues 513)

Property sharing was also done on a grade system like to a married daughter who had a son would get preference over a married woman, then a married woman, then a girl, then a widow. Ambedkar clarified the doubts raised by some members in the House and concluding his speech over the Hindu Code Bill in the parliament said: "I think I have, so far as I know, exhausted what I have to say on the various points of controversy which I had seen raised both by members of this House as well as by the members of the public. I hope that the clarification which I have given on the various points will allay the fears of members who are not well disposed towards this measure. They will realize that this is in no sense a revolutionary measure. I say that this is not even a radical measure." (Rodrigues 516)

Because the Bill was on uniformity of Law it was very dear to Ambedkar. But as tradition rules over thoughts on equality for man and woman, his thoughts on equality were not taken positively and also not accepted for which he had to face much opposition. To express his dissatisfaction over this Ambedkar resigned from the post of Law Minister from Nehru's cabinet.

One of the main considerations which led to the codification of Hindu laws pertaining to women is that some of them placed women at a disadvantage as compared with men. But the bill met with stiff opposition. Orthodox Hindus abhorred the very idea of Ambedkar, an untouchable, piloting this bill. Ambedkar also realized that most of the prominent Indian women leaders were really not interested in the social progress of women. In spite of his concerted effort, Ambedkar could not succeed in putting the Hindu Code Bill on the status book. In this connection Ambedkar declared in relation to the significance of the Hindu Code Bill, "No law passed by the Indian Legislature in the past or likely to be passed in the future can be compared to it (Hindu Code) in terms of its significance. To leave inequality between class and class, between sex and sex which is the soul of Hindu society, untouched and to go on passing legislation relating to economic problems is to make a farce of our Constitution and to build a palace on a dung heap. This is the significance I attached to the Hindu Code." (BAWS 14, part 1, p. i)

Ambedkar who considered development of women as a part of his reform movement also thought that women could get equality only when some laws are made in their favour. He was a man who acted on the issues which he felt would help women in their development so he drafted The Hindu Code Bill which was most vehemently resisted in the parliament. His emphasis in his argument on the bill was to reform Hinduism and to create a large enough public space regulated by rule of law applicable to one and all. He was open to diversity but only under the rule of law. The orthodoxy clearly perceived a threat from the bill, but even those who supported Ambedkar did not do it for the reasons he stressed. Some of them saw it from its fissiparous tendencies, buttressing their viewpoint. Further while Ambedkar sought integral and holistic changes in the Hindu Code, his opponents insisted on 'piecemeal' change. While explaining his stand over the Hindu Code Bill Ambedkar highlighted the major provisions of the Bill. However, given the kind of challenges the Bill faced, he made defence of the Bill by underplaying its radical edge and linking it with the *shastras*, usages, customs and simple reasonableness.

Ambedkar's ideas and concept of life are reflected in his speeches and the Indian constitution. He was the person to realize that if Indian society has to improve, an awareness has to be created, bringing gender into the focus of discussion. He declared that by bringing a gender consciousness to civil and political, as well as social and economic rights, women's emancipation is possible. It should be noted that Gandhi introduced women into the ongoing freedom struggle, but Ambedkar added two more things into it. He said that the social and economic development also needs a thorough change by a change in the attitude towards women and their emancipation. But the nation was not enthusiastic about such movements and he was opposed inside and outside the Parliament because the society and its leaders were not in a position to appreciate the progressive outlook of Ambedkar and his principle of social justice, which is based upon equality, liberty and fraternity, and which considered human rights the fundamental principle of a cultured society.

Our constitution is regarded as one of the best in the world and through it Ambedkar has expressed his commitment to the women's cause. The most important contribution of Dr. Ambedkar was his fight for equal rights for women and for their voting rights. Indian constitution granted voting rights to women as a right. American women and women in other western countries like England, France and other European Countries, had to fight for their voting rights for decades before they were allowed to vote. Our constitution also grants equality to women in property.

As India's first Law Minister and Chairman of the Drafting Committee of his Constituent Assembly, Ambedkar tried to relieve women from the age-old atrocities by reforming the Hindu laws codified by Manu. He on 'Hindu Code' Parliamentary Debates dated 26 September 1951, explained: "In our constitution we adopted a middle course; the course that we adopted was this, that while we will permit people to participate and to profess their religion and incidentally, to have their personal law because the personal law is so embedded in their religion, yet the state has retained all along in article 25 the right to interfere in the personal law of any community in this country. There can be no argument about that. . . . Let no community be in a state of mind that they are immune from the sovereign authority of this parliament." (BAWS 15, 2949) As rightly said by Nalini, Ambedkar moved towards a new social order by introducing the progressive and the secular into the constitution and thus declared a war against gender bias. He categorically announced before the world of men who dominated the political scene that during that period justice, equality, liberty in the sphere of public life should be the lifeline for our development. All are equal before law and justice. Caste, creed, religion, or sex will not come in the way of justice and the constitution would protect the rights of the individual (Nalini 129). While drafting the constitution, he was the prime mover of provisions related to the welfare of women. The constitutional debates are testimonies of his concern for the emancipation of women.

Besides providing constitutional guarantees to women, Dr. Ambedkar introduced and got passed four acts which strengthened the position of women in the society. These were incorporated in the Hindu Code Bill; they are: The Hindu Marriage Act, 1955, The Hindu Succession Act, 1956, The Hindu Minority and Guardianship Act 1956, The Adoption and Maintenance Act 1956.

A few articles in the constitution helped the women to improve their status and to compete with their male counterparts. For example, under Article 14 the state guarantees equality before law and equal protections of law to all citizens within the Indian Territory. Article 15 states that the state shall not discriminate against any citizen on grounds of religion, race, caste, sex, place of birth or any of them. Article 16 says there shall be equality of opportunity for all citizens in matters relating to employment or appointment to any office under the state. Under Article 29 the state grants all citizens, both men and women, equal rights to have adequate means of livelihood and Article 39(d) states that there is equal pay for both men and women. As per Article 41, the state shall guarantee within its economic limits to all the citizens, the right to work, to education, and public assistance in certain cases. Under Article 42 the state makes provision for just and human conditions of work and maternity relief and under Article 44, the state provides the uniform civil code to all the citizens throughout the territory of India.

The Indian constitution speaks of three kinds of justice—social, economic and political and then mentions three principles—liberty of thought, expression, belief, faith and worship; equality of status and opportunity; and fraternity, to ensure the dignity of the individual and the unity and integrity of the nation.

Once Ambedkar remarked that in an ideal society there should be many interests consciously communicated and shared. There should be social endosmosis. He was of the opinion that "lost rights are never regained by begging, but by relentless struggle". It is for this struggle that he prepared a ground in the Constitution and made the Judiciary the custodian to protect the rights. This shows how clear he was with his project and firm in his act that he gave the rights to women as a weapon in written form.

Therefore, long before anyone could think of equality and equal status and opportunity for women in the male dominated society, and where religious and social beliefs of all sorts created an atmosphere of insecurity and fear in the minds of women,

Ambedkar started a crusade against social injustice that had brought havoc in the society in the name of religion and custom.

Ambedkar, through the various clauses of the Indian constitution, aimed at promoting change in social and economic structures so that it would ensure full equality of women and greater participation in the development process without discrimination, national strategies and constitutional and legislative guarantee of the principle of non-discrimination, and equal opportunities in education and work are achieved. He gave alternatives to society. By burning the *Manusmriti* he gave a Constitution based on equality to all, irrespective of caste, creed and gender. Ambedkar described himself as a progressive radical and occasionally as a progressive conservative. He not only acted against inequality but also gave an alternative to society. He gave a weapon to the women of India to fight for their rights by using constitutional means. The preamble of the constitution says: "We the people of India have solemnly resolved to constitute India a sovereign, socialist, democratic republic." In 1950, he turned to Buddhism as a new personal faith and as an ideology that offered an alternative to Hinduism. The purpose of his accepting other religions was his search for equality which he found missing in Hinduism. He accepted Buddhism because its base was on equality and he found equality of women and the lower status of people here for which he fought throughout his life. Through his discourses he challenged power positions by representing reality and social relations in a new society. His influence on women's movement is still visible and his impact on the discursive dimension of Indian English prose is immense. His achievement was to give a new orientation to attitudes of men and women towards each other, thus bringing about a new respect in the arena of gender relations. Therefore, Ambedkar's discourse is a very significant one in any discussion on women's emancipation in India.

Conclusion

In a seminal volume entitled Discourse David Howarth suggests some extremely relevant pointers to discourse analysis applicable to the four male voices chosen for study in this book . He says: "saying something [is] . . . also doing something . . . speakers adopt certain 'speaker roles' . . . certain ritualized words . . . these insights enable us to understand patterns of individual relations between interactants, individuals' position within larger institutional structures, and overall 'social organization.'" (6-7) Citing Fairclough's insistence on the social dimension of discourse and its analysis, he further says: "there is a mutually constituting relationship between discourse and the social systems in which they function." (4) He also suggests: "discourses constitute symbolic systems and social orders and the task of discourse analysis is to examine their historical and political construction and functioning." (5)

The four chapters have taken up numerous examples of passages from the four reformers in order to show the distinctive nature of their discourse, which individually and collectively—raised the issue of women's role in society and achieved some degree of success in women's emancipation.

The discourse for the liberation of women has changed because today women are empowered and they can raise their voice for their own rights. They have the constitutional rights, they are educated and there is an increase in their awareness is created through the print and electronic media. This change has come in Indian women's movement of the present day through two phases—the early efforts of the male reformers and the resultant women's movements in the hands of some privileged women of today.

There is a sharp distinction between the character of the women's movement of earlier times and today. During the nineteenth and the early part of the twentieth century, the initiative and leadership of women's reforms came from men. Women remained only as mute spectators, and it seemed inconceivable that women could ever come out of their cloistered homes to demand reforms. They were fully dependent on men even for their own welfare. In the modern world, the scene has changed significantly. It is very significant to note that women's voice which are no longer stifled; a large number of women are actively expressing their problems and asking for solutions following in the footsteps of the early efforts for the emancipation of women by male social reformers

The reformers of the 19th century fought against the legal and social evils to which Indian women were being subjected, but did not fight to elevate women to the same level as that of men. At their time, for the reformers, the survival of women was more important as they wanted to save Hindu women from social evils and oppression in the society. But the most significant characteristic features of the present-day women's movement in India are women fighting for their rights themselves and secondly, their demand is for equal opportunity in all fields. A distinct discourse has therefore governed the various stages of the evolution of women's emancipation movement. In this context three crucial parameters and their interrelated nature are the frames of references: discourse, language and social practice. As Tern A. van Dijk says: "Discourse . . . is also a practical, social and cultural phenomenon . . . language users engaging in discourse accomplish social acts and participate in social interaction, . . . such interaction is in turn embedded in various social and cultural contexts." (1997: 2)

As has been noted earlier, discourse refers to language use as social practice. Discourse is both constitutive and constituted. Discourse is the kind of language used within a specific field such as political or scientific discourse. It also refers to a way of speaking which gives meaning to experience from a particular perspective. Knowledge is created through social interaction in which we construct common truths and compete about what is true and false. All these are comparable issues when talking about the four reformers chosen for study in this book . From Roy through Phule, Gandhi to Ambedkar, the backdrop for their ideas and expressions depended largely on the social climate of their times. Therefore the language they used was also determined by social concerns. Each of them had a distinct discourse but in many places their individuality merged with the requirements of the common issues—that is, women's empowerment.

As a guide to all the women of the depressed class he advised them to improve their living conditions because keeping themselves neat and clean, giving education to their children and teaching their children to develop confidence and improve their lives will help them to change their living standards. All the women took his advice seriously because they learnt that whatever he said was true. They found him as their messiah who was struggling to improve their lives and also raise them in statues society.

> I shall tell you a few things which I think you should bear in mind. Learn to be clean; keep free from all vices. Give education to your children. Instill ambition in them. Inculcate in their minds that they are destined to be great. Remove from them all inferiority complexes. Don't be in a hurry to marry: marriage is a liability. You should not impose it on your children unless financially they are able to meet the liabilities arising from marriage. Those who will marry will bear in mind that to have too many children is a crime. That parental duty lies in giving each child a better start than its parents had. (BAWS 17, part 3, 282-83)

Ambedkar expressed these views on marriage to the women at the meeting. His view was that, their children are economically independent they should not think of marriage at all. He also said that producing many children was not the duty of the parents but to give them a good and respectable living was more important. Like a father, he advised them on every topic to make their home a happy home. The most important advice he gave to women was to be on an equal footing with their husband and not subordinate to him or a slave.

Above all, let each girl who marries stand up to her husband, claim to her husband as equal, and refuse to be a slave. I am sure if you follow this advice you will bring honor and glory to yourself and to Depressed Classes. (BAWS 17, part 3, 283)

The above speech reflects his understanding of the basic problems of the women of depressed classes; keeping themselves clean, educating the children, and inculcating in their minds that they are destined to be great, not to be in a hurry to marry, being a friend to their husbands and not slaves—all this shows how much concern he had for their cause. We can see the softness in his address to the poor people, compared to the erudite and strong writings in English. He built confidence in them for their progress. This speech can be looked into as confidence-building even today to the depressed class because unless a person develops confidence in himself it is not possible for his progress. Ambedkar's advice was imbibed by the women word by word and they strove for their progress which was kept away from them for many years in the name of religion. With this confidence, the Dalit women were able to participate in all fields along with other women for their progress.

Roy was conversant with many languages; Sanskrit, Arabic, Persian, Hindūstani, Bengali, English, Hebrew, Greek, Latin and French. Ambedkar knew Sanskrit, English, Marathi, Hindi, and Konkani. Ambedkar was denied the opportunity to learn Sanskrit in India. He learnt it in Germany. He did so to understand why this inequality was observed in Hindu society. Phule knew Modi, Hindi, Marathi and English. Gandhi knew Sanskrit, English, Gujrati and Hindi. Being multilingual helped them to understand the problems and to remain in close contact with the people. Roy and Phule concentrated on the Regional/state level whereas Gandhi and Ambedkar took the issue to the national level. This was not only due to the prevalent English education but also the nationalistic colour of the freedom movement which made their platform nationwide. The reformers changed themselves according to the needs of the audience while addressing them. They were polemic while addressing the common people and erudite addressing the educated people. This helped them in making people understand their project of women's emancipation.

The reformers selected are not of the same time but the styles of their discourse was similar. For instance, the dialogue form was adopted by Rammohun Roy and Phule. They adopted the method of writing their ideas in a dialogic structure to make people understand their ideology. They even introduced Samajs like Brahmo Samaj by Rammohun Roy and Satyasodhak Samaj by Phule to freely express their ideas without any restrictions because opposing the tradition while being in it was difficult. The print media which was introduced by the British was a boon to the Indians. Rammohun Roy, Gandhi and Ambedkar started their own newspapers to express their thoughts and educate people about their ideologies. Their newspapers were in local languages because their mission was to send the message to the common people. Take for example; the newspaper started by Ambedkar was named as *Mooknayak* which means hero of the dumb. The name itself gave a kind of assurance to the people who were suffering under the name of religion that there is someone to listen to them and address their problems.

Roy made the best use of the English language to communicate his ideas, by doing a deep study of English in the twenty-second year of his life. He became competent to converse freely on the most abstruse subjects and to argue more closely and coherently than most men he knew. He brought out a journal published in the language of the common people, conducted by themselves, designed for the perusal of Indians. He wrote simple and lucid Hindi and his command over the language was testified by the eminent critic Pandit Hazari Prasad Dwivedi. Roy published the Hindi translation of *Vedanta Sutra* in 1815. Roy wanted English education but he also wanted the education system to be perfectly on the lines of and in consonance with the religious dictum. Any educational policy or system, which was free from religious control, was never supported by Roy. His strong views were that religion must play a significant role in structuring the education system.

Discourse contributes to the construction of social identities, social relations and system of knowledge and meaning. It functions as an 'identity', a 'relation' and an 'ideational'.

In the Indian system caste plays a very important role. The impact of the types of discourse used by a person also depends on the caste of a particular person. Applying this parameter to the four reformers is interesting: Rammohun Roy was from the Brahmin, Phule from the Mali community, Gandhi from the Baniya community and Ambedkar from the Mahar community. The utterances of the reformers had its authority according to their caste. Roy was accepted in spite of his opposing the tradition because of his caste. Roy was associated mostly with the upper class of the society. He opposed the tradition but not the religion. So he concentrated only on the issues relating to problems. Raja Rammohun Roy's view on the education policy also appears to be very progressive and aware. Roy spoke of filtration in the system of education for women by saying if women of upper castes were educated first naturally it would reach to the women of other castes. Phule did not differentiate between upper or lower castes because he knew the pain of discrimination. He took the problem as a problem of all Indian women irrespective of their *varna* or caste and addressed it accordingly. Gandhi wanted some changes in the Hindu tradition but overall his discourse was justification of Hindu religion. Ambedkar wanted a complete change in the system to bring a change in the emancipatory movement of the Indian women.

Raja Rammohun Roy's contribution to female emancipation in colonial India relates to the awareness that he has created over the inhuman social practice of *sati*, through the tracts which were his translations of the Vedic texts from the original Sanskrit to

Bengali in order to first enable the common man to understand that the sacred scripture has not allowed the inhuman practice of *sati*. Then, he again translated it into English to make the British colonial rulers realize that there was nothing religious about the evil practice of s*ati* so that they could contemplate the enactment of a suitable law to abolish *sati*.

In this context it is pertinent to observe that Raja Rammohun Roy went to England in order to defend his stand against *sati* in the court of England. A group of hundred Hindu priests who were staunch supporters of *sati* and who opposed Roy, sent a letter to the judge of the court of England maintaining that Roy posted himself to be a potential threat to Hindu religion. Despite such a plea, Roy in the court defended the abolition of the evil practice of *sati*. Roy argued that it was hypocrites who had made such laws for their own self-aggrandizement in order to perpetuate the male dominance to have control over the property of the deceased husband if woman was made a *sati*. He also pleaded that no holy scripture had supported the evil practice of *sati*.

Thus, Roy's opinions influenced the minds of the people at large and the colonial rulers as well in such a way that they led them to an effective action and in turn to a desired change in Indian society. His contribution, therefore, to women's emancipation consists in his tracts, speeches, arguments and writings, all assuming the dimensions of a powerful discourse for a social purpose.

Roy opposed tradition not religion. He believed in one god. He started the Brahmo Samaj to spread his message, but as tradition dominates the society in the name of religion, Roy had to face opposition. In spite of addressing many issues he concentrated mostly on *sati* which was considered as one of the cruel acts on women in the name of religious customs and traditions. He worked on it until a law was passed banning this crime. He decided to take up this cause when he saw his sister-in-law commit sati. Roy wrote in English simultaneously with Bengali. This was a plus point for his ideas to be conveyed to many, especially the

British rulers. It is here that questions relating to change and ideological consequences are addressed. The questions raised are: i) whether the discursive reproduces the order of discourse and thus maintains the status quo in the social change, ii) what the ideological, political and social consequences of the discursive practice are, iii) whether the discursive practice conceals and strengthens unequal power relations in society, or iv) whether it challenges power positions by representing reality and social relations in a new way.

The above is pertinently relevant to Dr. Ambedkar's contribution to female emancipation in colonial India. His main contribution lies in the fact that he had waged a relentless fight against casteism in general and the pernicious social practice of untouchability rampantly prevalent in Indian society during his days. His western education coupled with his extraordinary intellectual abilities largely helped him realize the unequal power relations in society that existed between caste Hindus and Dalits. He vehemently opposed Manu, the Hindu law giver, and the scriptures that Manu had evolved whereby a particular section of Indian society to whom all rights and opportunities—social, economic, educational, political and religious—were denied for centuries. On the other hand, his knowledge of the pathetic conditions of Indian women in general and the Dalit women in particular made him challenge the power position of the dominant caste Hindus by representing reality and social relations in a new way. His enormous legal knowledge and his command over international and constitutional matters enabled him in two ways. He drafted the Hind Code Bill and presented it in the Indian Parliament and his successful endeavour to incorporate the reservations to the scheduled castes and the scheduled tribes in the third schedule of the Indian constitution for educational and employment opportunities. The Hindu Code Bill was intended to give women equality with men in unified civil code, divorce, adoption, property rights in father's property along with son.

Ambedkar's observation about the downfall of Indian women is praiseworthy. The maintenance of strict endogamy for surplus men and surplus women was the main challenge. Here he also noted that man being powerful and having an upper hand in society cannot be forcibly controlled. Thus, society left him untouched; but women being considered inferior to men were easy prey of victimization. So a 'protective' measure, *Sati*, system was introduced, whereby a surplus woman i.e. a widow, was forced to burn herself along with her deceased husband. But in some cases it was difficult to operate so the second remedy was to compulsorily enforce widowhood on her for rest of her life, and in order to guard her morals and also the morals of a group, the widows were obliged to follow much restrictions such as shaven head, restriction on diets, wearing of colorless sari and no intermixing with anyone in order to ensure that they were no longer sources of allurement.

As said above, both these treatments—*sati* and enforced widowhood were not possible in the case of surplus man because of his domination. Therefore, surplus man was allowed to re-marry to recruit another bride, but in this situation, there was every possibility of decreasing number of women available among the so-called upper castes therefore, as a corrective measure, a man was allowed to choose his wife from lower marriageable rank, and this resulted in the beginning of Girl-child Marriage. In this way, the inhuman practices of *sati* system enforced widowhood and child marriage came into existence. Thus, much before the Indian feminist schools, Dr. Ambedkar pointed out that there is a direct relationship between caste and gender and put forward a very fundamental and original observation that gender could not be seen in isolation from caste.

Ambedkar's principal contribution also rests on his role as the chairman of the Drafting Committee of the Indian Constitution. If Manu was regarded as the Hindu law giver; .Ambedkar has a greater claim to be regarded as the maker of the Indian Constitution. While drafting the constitution he incorporated the three cardinal principles namely liberty, equality and fraternity for all Indians into every article of the Constitution.

Ambedkar's contribution to women's emancipation also owes its strength to his innate faith in equality of gender in Indian society in spite of age-old cultural, social and religious constraints. Discourse revolves round three processes—thinking, perception and reasoning.

Ambedkar's contempt for casteism and his opposition to Hinduism culminated in his embracing Buddhism. Because he strongly believed that Buddhism, unlike Hinduism, would provide equality to all men and women in general and help in the emancipation of women in particular. His writings, speeches and debates assuming all the dimensions of discourses influenced the minds of people of his day and made them follow his path. Thus Ambedkar opposed the tradition which he said was part of religion.

He has to his credit more writing than speeches which have become a guide for many for further analyzing the problems. Whatever he wrote, it was written with historical facts/proofs and he very confidently justified whatever he said and wrote. As he hailed from the deprived sections of society, he was aware of the problem of discrimination and so he included women of all sections of society in his fight for equality. He fought for the equality of rights and human dignity for the untouchables of the society in which he included women also. The for him when he got the opportunity to write the Indian Constitution he saw to it that women were not shown discrimination and he wrote in the preamble of the constitution that all men and women are equal before law. He gave women the weapon of law to fight for their equality. He had to face much opposition from the society because he strongly condemned all the traditions and customs which, according to him, have brought discrimination into society.

Gandhi's contribution to women's emancipation in colonial India are concerned, with that dimension of discourse which involves cognitive psychology. Cognitive psychology ascribes to the modern conception of the individual as an autonomous delimited agent with a set of authentic characteristics. The individual and society are regarded as separate entities. It implies the existence of dualism between the individual and society.

Gandhi's approach to women's emancipation suffered from various potential pitfalls. Gandhi encouraged women to take part in mass movements in the freedom struggle, but when he organized Salt Satyagraha, and Dandi march he wanted the women to be away from the march because he did not want to be labeled as taking the help of women. However, a small number of women took part in Salt Satyagraha under the leadership of Sarojini Naidu. Gradually Gandhi changed his attitude towards women and as part of their emancipation, he called them to come out of their homes in order to participate in the freedom struggle as he felt that India could win political freedom only through united strength of both men and women. As a result, Indian women started participating in the non-cooperation movement. One of the more comprehensive and sophisticated critiques of Gandhi has come from Madhu Kishwar. A lengthy and detailed analysis of Gandhi's writings convinces her of the fact that Gandhi used contrastively the traditional symbols, highlighting their positive characteristic, to effectively push women into participating in the political movement.

Gandhi worked for the abolition of the evil practice of untouchability and child marriage. He also worked for the development of women through education. He took the stand of religion for the liberation of women. He had dual opinions and changed his talk depending on the situation. He also was very clear of what he meant and clarified the doubts of the people when he was asked for clarification or advice. He considered marriage as sacred and remarriage of a widow or widows unthinkable and improper. Later he was of the opinion that widows should be remarried in case the marriage had not been consummated before the death of the husband. When he was questioned about this, he replied "the word 'remarriage is a misnomer in such cases. The virgin was never married at all in the true sense and, therefore, on the death of her supposed husband, it would be the most natural thing, it would be a duty, for the parents." (*Young India*, 26 September 1929)

He was a motherly figure to many people. They wrote letters to him about their problems and Gandhi often replied to all the letters. In one such letter a correspondent requested for advice about the marriage of a seventeen years old girl who had lost in Quetta is her husband, father-in-law, brother-in-law and the only child. In this context, Gandhi replied: "I do not know what my pen or voice can do in matters in which age-long prejudices are concerned. I have repeatedly said that every widow has as much right to marry as a widower. Voluntary widowhood is a boon in Hinduism; enforced widowhood is a crime . . . the girl who may have become widow in the natural course, will also find it easy to get married, if they are willing to do so." (*Harijan* 22 June 1935)

We see much matter on women's emancipation in Gandhi's writings and letters which he had written to different people. His writings in *Young India*, his autobiography *The Story of My Experiments with Truth*, his speeches and his interviews constituting a distinct form of discourse moved the minds of millions of women to fruitful action for achieving India's freedom and their constitutional rights.

Gandhi distrusted reason more than most modern moral and political thinkers in the west. He stressed on the limits of reason, regarded ahimsa as a 'matter not of the intellect but of the heart' and felt that in general men are ultimately guided not by the intellectual but by the heart: 'the heart accepts a conclusion for which the intellect subsequently finds the reasoning. Argument follows or wants to do'. Gandhi was bent upon bringing in the attitude of men towards women within the framework of Indian social ethos. Women as a group were guided by him for political reasons, though; he was really concerned with their welfare and position in Indian society.

With his weapon of non-violence Gandhi was successful in bringing women from the private to the public domain. The thought came to him to fight against discrimination when he faced discrimination in South Africa. His guidance made women confident and impelled them to join the freedom struggle; they were impressed by his appeal to women to come out and fight for the freedom movement. The simplicity of Gandhi attracted many because most of the women came from rural backgrounds. An advantage for Gandhi was that by this time some women were educated and some awareness had been created in them so that they had also started to question the tradition. He took the examples of Sita and Damyanti and praised the tradition and the women of India compared to women of any other country. He argued that man and woman are the creation of God and the distribution of labour was the man going out to work and woman looking after the house. He always justified the dignity of labour and discouraged the fight for equality. He did not face opposition because without opposing tradition, he saw to it that change can be brought about. This was his achievement.

Jyotirao Phule's contribution can be seen in the fact that his domain of activities was more action-oriented than in verbal utterance. Phule was a man of practical wisdom. He preached what he practiced and practiced what he preached. His multifarious activities included singing ballads, staging street plays, circulating pamphlets, writing on the wall, all these activities aimed at bringing about the improvement of education for the downtrodden in general and women in particular. His role as a social reformer mainly lies in his establishing schools for women. He educated his wife and made her a teacher. His vehement opposition to brahminization of education abetted by the scriptures molded his fierce personality. His own experience of having been humiliated and insulted by Brahmin elders when he participated in the marriage procession of his Brahmin friend totally changed his attitude and behaviour towards Indian society after which he waged a relentless battle against all sorts of injustices that were meted out to the people of the downtrodden communities.

Phule fought for the cause of widow marriage. He established a foundling home for those widows who became pregnant.

Kashibai's suicide deeply moved him. He secretly gave shelter to many such Brahmin widows and saved them from committing suicide.

Phule not only opposed tradition but he said that the cause of this tradition is religion. He hails the deprived sections of society. He commented vehemently and critically on religious priests. This was not acceptable to many and he had to face great opposition at his time. He wrote mostly in Marathi which was his mother tongue and therefore his communication in that language was more powerful and revolutionary than in English which he used only for appeals and requests pertaining to thought provoking issues. Because of the use of language which was regional his thoughts were restricted only to the people of Maharashtra. In spite of his thoughts being very modern and revolutionary, his action in implementation of his ideas had great opposition from society, as tradition played a very important role. Nevertheless, he was successful in practicing what he preached.

Phule's action-oriented discourse led to ideas and these ideas eventually translated themselves into action by the people. Their action led to change. The process of change led to emancipation. Phule's discourse helps in understanding the impact of oral communication even in the present-day world, its social influence and the transformation it brought about in the minds and mannerisms of the listeners.

Ambedkar on the other hand privileged the written word. He would make written submissions before committees and commissions to negotiate across the authority of a formulated text. In a culture that was largely oral, the written word enabled him to reach out to a larger world, conferring some degree of permanence or immortality and allowing him to usurp some of the Brahmanical authority. The writings, therefore, cannot be separated from their nexus to power, though they are caught in their quest for power, in variegated ways, some in the immediate sense and others with permanent implications. This nexus can insinuate the significance of a text differently from other writings.

Sometimes, Ambedkar made a text about the battleground where, massaging his troops, he launched an attack on the 'enemy territory', the adversary text or point. The way he handled *Manusmriti, Bhagavad Gita* are apt illustrations of this. Ambedkar thought that winning these battles was crucial for reformulating social relations. He became deeply aware of the resources that history and culture offered for an emancipatory project but argued that they can become effective only through the matrix of the present. Undoubtedly he had the highest academic credentials for an India of his time, and his erudition and scholarship have been widely acknowledged. He deployed its concepts, cited its authority and negotiated with the world, voicing a variety of subject matters. He traversed a forbidding grooming in liberal education of varied specialized areas such as history, economics, anthropology, politics and law, which imparted multifaceted resources and orientations to him. In his public life, Ambedkar was observed in several roles: a scholar, teacher, lawyer, parliamentarian, administrator, journalist, publicist, negotiator, agitationist, leader and devotee. It is difficult to demarcate the area of his writings given the fact that Ambedkar resorted to various modes of expressions—dissertations, research papers, documents outlines, notes, early drafts, statements, beliefs, memoranda, disputations and investigations—as he was often under pressure to play these roles always under the public eye.

Ambedkar delivered speeches for various occasions and at different forums, from the Constituent Assembly to mobilizational gatherings. Ambedkar himself gave a great deal of importance to writing compared to several other activities, including speaking, that men of his generation, background and erudition indulged in. He carefully planned the outlines of a text. He ascribed a great deal of authority to his own texts and combated with characteristic vehemence those he considered inimical to his perspective. We find extended quotations drawn from relevant texts including those of the adversary, to buttress his argument. This is particularly the case when the theme is related to the S*hastras*. In combative encounters with Brahminism, which he believed tended to monopolize learning and knowledge, he demonstrated not merely his own erudition but through a double reversal argued that true learning and knowledge, is different from what Brahminism upheld. In 1950 he turned to Buddhism as his personal faith and as an ideology that offered an alternative to Hinduism. Ambedkar described himself as a progressive radical and occasionally as a 'progressive conservative'.

Phule's activities extended beyond the field of education. He believed that revolutionary thought had to be backed by revolutionary praxis. He can be cited as an example of a long-line of nineteenth century reformers who had sensitively thought about the gender question. For Phule, it was the matter of praxis and revolution. Phule and his Satyasodhak Samaj founded in 1873 began their activity at the lower end of the social spectrum. This activity took Phule to all corners of western Maharashtra addressing meetings of shudras. Phule's vision, and scope of the Samaj's activity, was broad and with sweeping vision. There was virtually no aspect of social life that did not engage his attention.

Phule's world of ideas enabled him to have this broad sweeping vision and become the system-building personality that he was. The centre of Phule's thought is dharma and caste. His opposition to Brahmanism did not relate only to the varna system. It is also related to almost everything within the Hindu system. Phule rarely uses the term Hindu or Hinduism. He refers to brahminism instead. He was convinced that s*hrutis* (the Vedas) and the s*mritis* were a part of the brahmanical attempt at creating texts which would rationalize and perpetuate their dominance. Phule rejected this pseudo-religion along with the texts that upheld it. Phule was not interested in tinkering with that aspect of the brahmanical structure which he did not subscribe to, to make it a little more humane. He argued for its complete rejection and destruction. In its place, he sought to create dichotomous conceptions of the Hindu social structure. Ambedkar was also of the same opinion. Roy and Gandhi were of the opinion that only internal changes would work out for reform in Hindu society. It is because of this they both did not have much opposition from society like Phule and Ambedkar. Obviously, the ideological impact on their chosen discourse was mainly governed by this difference in their approaches.

Manu's system treats women—all women irrespective of varna—as *shudra* or *dasa*. Accordingly, Phule included women, all women, in his notion of shudratishudra. He did not think of women's problems in terms of Brahmin or shudra ati shudra. Phule did not talk of patriarchy. Nor did he give us a theory of man-woman inequality. He related some of the negatives of women's position to the *Arya-bhat* (literally priest) social order. Though he does not say so explicitly, he seems to imply that the end of the *Arya-bhat* domination would ensure man-woman equality. For him, a Brahmin woman was as much a shudra woman. In that sense, it was a remarkable modern and gendered view, which saw gender itself, as the basis for the oppression that women faced. He was only one who raised his voice against the near-hysterical reaction to Tarabai Shinde, who had published in 1882 what was called in today's language a feminist tract on *A Comparison Between Women and Men* (*Stree Purush Tulana*).

Phule's prose, his use of 19th century colloquial speech, his system of argumentation, his ferocious polemics, his poetry, his assessment of various Bhakti poets amounts to the beginning of Marathi socio-literary criticism. All these are aspects of his work which hardly, if ever, get discussed. Phule was very fond of the dialogue form. The use of dialogue connected him with the western, especially Greek tradition. Phule's language is remarkable, and, for his time, unique. Phule was trying to build a movement of the oppressed, and was trying through his writings to first and foremost reach out to those masses. It is then only to be expected that he speaks their language when he addresses them. But Phule goes a step further. His use of Marathi remains unconventional (for his times) even when he does not write for mass circulation. In the sense, Phule seems to be remolding the language itself, and asserting that the real Marathi is not the Sanskritized Marathi of the Brahmans, but that which draws from the language of the masses. (Deshpande 17)

Phule and Roy shared their preference for the dialogic form of discourse. They have some ideological similarities too. Roy felt that one of the major reasons for the prevalence of sati was the utter destitution to which women were reduced after the death of their husbands. According to Roy the ancient law-givers unanimously awarded to a mother an equal share with her sons in the property left by her deceased husband, in order that she spent her remaining days independently of her children. But the laws had been misinterpreted and abused, depriving widows and daughters of their share in the property of their husbands and fathers. When we look into the discourses of Ambedkar, he felt that women are the gateways to the caste system. All the cruel practices like *sati,* child marriage, widowhood, were to keep women under control. They not only came out with their reasons for the downfall of women they argued through their polemic as well as erudite writings and speeches in a lot of languages to make the educated and also the common people understand the reasons behind this problem and act accordingly. Orthodox Hindu reactions to these developments were not slow to come, and were considerably stronger. One of the reasons for this was that Brahman power-structures were far stronger. On a few occasions, the social reformers were threatened for their life. Phule, who was more involved in action-oriented activities, faced enormous hostility from caste Hindus for his presumption in attempting to raise the status of untouchables and women. Under pressure from the conservative Brahmins, his father threw him out of his home, and he was ostracized by many members of his own community. Roy was also made to leave his house when he challenged the social conditions. He had to face opposition from his own mother and was also not given his share in the property.

To challenge the power structure the reformers not only opposed the prevailing system but gave to the people a new way.

Rammohun Roy and Phule challenged the brahmanical system and revolted by opening new organizations like Brahmo Samaj by Rammohun Roy and Satyasodhak Samaj by Phule to propagate their own ideology under the banner of their own samaj.

Gandhi and Ambedkar gave subtle weapons to women to face the challenges of societal dominance. Gandhi gave the weapon of non-violence and Ambedkar gave the weapon of the Indian Constitution with legal rights to all irrespective of gender.

As we have seen, no progressive discourse is accepted immediately by the society. It is very difficult to make a change for the betterment of society. If the change is also made slowly the dominance of few in the name of tradition and religion has again imposed the system through superstitious beliefs. Sometimes changes are accepted but radical changes are not welcomed. The patterns of discourse taken up for the study are not contemporary discourses but were of different times and according to the need of the hour, depending upon the severity of the problems. But all belong to the colonial period. Gandhi and Ambedkar have lived in independent India after the country got independence so their discourse bridges the colonial and postcolonial period.

Women's emancipation was taken up mostly by women after independence but the feminists themselves seemed to have held conflicting views on the subject: if some asserted that men and women were complementary, others asserted that they were the same. The tensions between notions of complementarily and notions of equality were, however, only to be articulated by the second wave of feminism in India in the 1970s.

The Hindu Code Bill which was drafted by Ambedkar the then Law Minister was heavily opposed by a number of women along with a number of influential Congressmen, including the then President of India, Rajendra Prasad, and Sardar Patel, in spite of few feminists and social reformers who welcomed the Bill. Ambedkar resigned in protest and there was an outcry from some feminists, but the Government took no further action on the question of a uniform Hindu Code, the outcry receded, and the matter was dropped. (Indu Prakash Singh 97-107).

As Gail Omvedt rightly points out the goal of women's emancipation should be to help build up women's liberation movements linked to the revolutionary struggles of the toiling masses—but their role in the process should be to present before the masses a political line of women's liberation, i.e., a line which links women's liberation to fight for revolution, and to spread this as much as possible among the masses of working women and men, rural women and middle classes and partly and union activists. (1)

The people who propounded the arguments in the form of polemic against the Indian feminist movement, accusing Indian feminists of being agents of modernity who were attempting to impose crass market-dominated views of equality and liberty on a society which once gave the noble, the self-sacrificing and spiritual the respect they deserve, but which is now being rapidly destroyed by the essentially selfish forces of the market. All three, moreover, defined these crass market-dominated views of equality and liberty as being drawn from the west, so Indian feminists stood accused of being Westernists, colonialists, cultural imperialists, and indirectly supporters of capitalist ideology. Whenever there is a radical change there is opposition from the society.

The power structure of the dominant few in the name of tradition and religion is so strong that once again the evils have started creeping and in 1987 Roop Kanwar's death as sati was supported. Kumkum Sangari has pointed out how the new palatial sati temples replay the act of sati through models of the woman, the dead man and the burning pyre: she shows, further, that the 'worship' of sati-dharma or sati is produced and controlled through commodification, for next to the new temples there are sati-memorial stones which lie neglected and worshiped. (Sangari 1988).

The process through which the incident of sati happened is a revealing one, for it sheds light on communal formations in India and shows how issues of gender can become central to these. At the policy-maker and intelligentsia level the major argument of the pro-sati camp was that if the state represented the people, then the Rajputs were people among whom *sati* was an ideal and a tradition and as such it should be recognized and legitimized. On the ground, however, it was a deliberate attempt to marginalize the Rajputs. The opponents of sati were presented as people who were using the issue as a cover to attack the Rajputs per se. The first, head priests of the major Hindu temples in such centers as Benaras and Puri, issued statements that *sati* represented one of the noblest elements not only of Rajput culture, but of Hinduism, and claimed scriptural sanction for this view. While reiterating the need to legitimize *sati,* the main thrust of their argument was that such issues came under their purview and not that of the state.

The tradition verses modernity argument entered this context in such a way as to further isolate the feminists. The bogey of modernism was so successfully created that the fact that *sati* was being used to create a 'tradition' went unrecognized despite feminist efforts to emphasize it. Tradition was defined so historically and so self-righteously that it obscured the fact that *sati* was being used to reinforce caste and communal identities along 'modern' lines, with modern methods of campaigning and organizing, modern arguments, and for modern ends, such as the reformation of electoral blocs and caste and communal representation within the state.

Today not only the tradition versus modernity argument is seen but the crime against women is increasing in many ways. Police records show high incidence of crimes against women in India. The National Crime Records Bureau reported in 1998 that the growth rate of crimes against women would be higher than the population growth rate by 2010.

In the twenty-first century one of the most valuable insights in this regard has been the understanding that while specific and short-term campaigns are necessary, if only in order to mark reactions, the roots of feminism are now spreading in a variety of ways of across the country. New reactions to feminist ideologies have emerged including a generation of male scholars involved in gender studies, (Kimmel 57-68)

The relationship between men and feminism has been complex. Men have taken part in significant responses to feminism in each 'wave' of the movement. There have been positive and negative reactions and responses, depending on the individual man and the social context of the time. (Lingard; Douglas*)*.

Women in India have achieved a new life for them where they can boast of revolutionary change in the approach to their problems. They have a status in public life. Many avenues are opening for them. They can work in many fields, their vote can sway election results, and education is expanding universally.

But, legal equality is one and equality in practice is another. Opportunities are still limited, as tradition continues to play the depressing role of reaction. Women are accused of rejecting their feminine role if they show interest in outside work.

Lack of sufficient education, especially among the rural women, is largely responsible for their lack of progress and confidence, and stands in the way of achieving economic independence, without which any hope of gaining equality inevitably withers away. So, as a reinforcement of governmental efforts, more private voluntary organizations should take up the task of educating the rural poor—men and women—and make them aware of the practical realities and the need for a radical change.

There is an urgent need for attitudinal revolution among women. There should be awareness among women about their miserable conditions and need to change. 'Women's Decade' has emphasized this proposition to a great extent. The modern women have to depend on their own ability to educate, organize and continue their struggle for all round development.

The movement is not complete because only social aspects were dealt with by the 19th century reforms and also because the weight of tradition is so strong and it is very difficult to change the mindset of the people who are completely dependent on tradition. So the inequality of women still prevails.

The 19th century emancipation was direct and there were limitations in the movement of the reformers at that time. But it has become very complex in the present context. The problem of women is not of women only but of the whole society. So it should be solved by both men and women. Taking empowerment as a movement in the present day we have to look into the past where men fought for women's emancipation and later women taking it up for their emancipation. Today the need of the hour is both coming together to fight for equality for all in society for a better living.

To get over the transitional period and become a modern state, we must spread scientific thinking on a massive scale, and encourage people to give up superstitions and backward feudal ideas like casteism and communalism. This is only possible by means of a complete revolution in our thinking and attitude towards women. What is needed is a massive cultural struggle involving hundreds of millions of people which will sweep away all remnants of the disgusting feudal and medieval practices and mentality, particularly with respect to women. These should be replaced with scientific thinking and genuine and complete equality between men and women.

Such a road-map is incipient in the speeches and writings of all the four reformers chosen for the study. Their words and actions have literary, sociological, cultural, political, psychological and gender-related relevance today because what they have said, the way they have said it, to whom they have said it and the social backdrop of their utterances continue to have overt and covert relevance in most of the issues related to women and gender roles. One of the aspects of discourse analysis and current research in areas of discourse highlights the question of gender in determining discursive patterns. From this perspective, the four personalities chosen for analysis provide valuable frames of reference with tremendous scope for further study and research.

Bibliography

Ahir, D.C. *Ambedkar and the Indian Constitution*. Lucknow: Buddha Vihar, 1973.

_____. *Dr. Ambedkar on Buddhism*. Bombay: Siddhartha, 1982.

_____. *The Legacy of Dr. Ambedkar*. Delhi: B.R., 1990.

Ahluwalia, B.K. and Shashi Ahluwalia. *B.R. Ambedkar and Human Rights*. New Delhi: Manas Publication, 1990.

Ahmed, Karuna. "*Gandhi, Women's Role and the Freedom Movement.*" *Occasional Papers,* New Delhi: Nehru Memorial Museum and Library. 1984..

Altekar, A.S. *The Position of Women in Hindu Civilization*. Benares: Motilal Banarasi Das, 1956.

Althusser, L. "Ideology and Ideological State Apparatuses." *Lenin and Philosophy and Other Essays.* London: New Left Review, 1971.

Ambedkar, B.R. *Dr. Babasaheb Ambedkar: Writings and Speeches (BAWS).* Vasant Moon, ed. Bombay: Government of Maharashtra Publication.1995. Vol. 1, 1979. Vol. 5, 1989. Vol. 14. Parliamentary debates, Vol, 15, p. 2949, dt. 26 September 1951. Vol. 17, 2003.

_____. *The Buddha and His Dhamma*. Bombay: Siddharth, 1957.

_____, *The Rise and Fall of Hindu Women*. Jalandhar: Bheem Patrika Publication, 1988.

Andrew, Charles. *Mahatma Gandhi's Ideas*. New York: Macmillian, 1930.

Ashe, Fidelma. *The New Politics of Masculinity.* London: Routledge,, 2004.

Asthana, Pratima. *Women's Movement in India*. New Delhi: Vikas, 1974.

Aurobindo, Sri. *The Foundations of Indian Culture and the Renaissance in India.* Vol 14, Pondicherry: Sri Aurobindo Ashram, 1971.

Baisantry, D.K. *Ambedkar, The Total Revolutionary*. New Delhi: Segment Book Distributors, 1991.

Balley, L.R., ed. *Ambedkar's Thoughts: Relevance of Ambedkar Mission*. Jalandhar: Buddhist Publishing House, 1983.

Bandyopadhyay, Sekhat. *Caste, Politics and the Raj: Bengal 1872-1937.* Calcutta: K.P. Bagchi, 1990.

Basham, A.L. *The Wonder That Was India*. New York: Grove, 1954.

Basu, Sharmita. *Religious Revivalism as Nationalist Discourse: Swami Vivekananda and New Hinduism in Nineteenth-Century Bengal.* Delhi: Oxford University Press, 2002.

Baxi, Upendra. "Emancipation as Justice: Legacy and Vision of Dr. Ambedkar." *From Periphery to Centre Stage: Ambedkar, Ambedkarism and Dalit Future*, ed. K.C. Yadav. Delhi: Manohar, 2000.

Bearce, George D. *British Attitudes towards India, 1784-1858*. Oxford: Oxford University Press, 1961.

Behera, D.K. "Social-Cultural Problems of the Christians of S.C." *Man & Life: Journal of the Institute of Social Research and Applied Anthropology* 15.1-2 1989.

Beteille, Andre. *Inequality and Social Change*. New Delhi: Oxford University Press, 1972.

Biswas, A.K. *Social and Cultural Vision of India*. Delhi: Pragati, 1996.

_____. *Sati: Saga of a Gory Practice*. New Delhi: Bloom Books, 1997.

Blommaert, *Discourse*: A Critical Introduction. Cambridge; Cambridge University Press, 2005.

Bloor, Meriel and Thomas Bloor. *The Practice of Critical Discourse Analysis,* an Introduction. London: Hodder Education Co., 2007.

Borman, William. *Gandhi and Non-Violence*. New York: State University N.Y. Press, 1986.

Brod, Harry. "To Be a Man, or Not to be a Man—That Is the Feminist Question," *Men Doing Feminism*, Tom Digby, ed. New York: Routledge, 1993.

Brown, Gilliam and George Yule, *Discourse Analysis*. Cambridge: Cambridge University Press, 1983.

Brailsford, H.N., 'Subject India 1943', qtd. A.N. Rajashekharaiah. *B.R. Ambedkar: The Politics of Emancipation*.

Chakravarti, Uma. *Rewriting History: The Life and Times of Pandita Ramabai.* New Delhi: Kali for Women, 1998.

_____. "From Exclusion to Marginalisation? Hegemonic Agendas and Women's Writings." *Thinking Social Science in India*, ed. Sujata Patel et al. Delhi: Sage, 2002.

_____. *The Social Dimensions of Earlier Buddhism*. Delhi: Munshiram

Manoharlal, 1996.

Chalam, K.S. *Education and Weaker Sections*. New Delhi: Inter-India, 1988.

Chandrama, S.K. *B.R. Ambedkar Writer Statesman: A Panoramic View,* New Delhi: CBS, 1995.

Chatterjee, Partha. *Nationalist Thought and the Colonial World: A Derivative Discourse*. Delhi: Oxford University Press, 1966.

Chatterji, Reena. *Impact of Raja Rammohun Roy on Education in India.* New Delhi: S. Chand, 1983.

Chouliaraki, Lilie and Norman Fairclough, *Discourse in Late Modernity*: Rethinking Critical Discourse Analysis. Edinburgh, Edinburgh University Press, 1999.

Coulthard, Malcolm, *An Introduction to Discourse Analysis*, (New Edition) Longman, 1985.

Crooke, Williams. *The Popular Religion and Folklore of Northern India*. Delhi: Munshiram Manoharlal, 1968.

Crowley, T. *Language in History: Theories and Texts*. London and New York: Routledge, 1996.

_____. *The Politics of Discourse: The Standard Language Question in British Cultural Debates.* London: Macmillan, 1988.

Dadhich, Naresh. *Gandhi and Existentialism*. Jaipur: Rawat, 1993.

Damodar, Balwant. *Buddha's India*: Essence of Buddhism Publication, 1991.

Dandavate, Madhu. "Dr. Ambedkar: A Dreamer of Social Liberation," *Pravartan. Siddharth College of Arts, Science and Commerce, Bombay, Golden Jubilee Commemorative Volume*. December 2002.

Das Gupta, B.N. *Raja Rammohun Roy: The Last Phase*. Delhi: Publishing House, 1980.

Datta, V.N. *Sati—Widow Burning in India*. Delhi: Manohar, 1988.

Dhaktode, S.S. "Dr. Ambedkar's Educational Philosophy," Pravartan. Siddharth College of Arts, Science and Commerce, Bombay: Golden Jubilee Commemorative volume. December, 2002.

Desai, Neera. *Women in India*. Bombay: Vora Publishers, 1957.

Deshpande, G.P., ed. *Selected Writings of Jyotirao Phule*. New Delhi: Naya Rastra Publishers, 2002.

Desai, A.R. *Social Background of Indian Nationalism.* 5th ed. Bombay: Popular Prakashan, 1991.

Devi, Lalitha. *Status and Employment of Women in India*. Delhi: B.R. Publishing Corporation, 1982.

Dubois, J.A., and H.K. Beauchamp. *Hindu Manners, Customs and Ceremonies*. Oxford: Clarendon Press, 1928.

Dumont, Louis. *Homo Hierarchicus: The Caste System and its Implications*. Chicago: The University of Chicago Press, 1972.

Edwards, D. and J. Potter. *Discursive Psychology*. London: Sage, 1992.

Everett, J.M. *Women and Social Change in India*. New Delhi: Heritage, 1979.

Fairclough, Norman. *Analysing Discourse*. Textual analysis for social research, London, Routledge, 2003.

_____. *Critical Language Awareness*. London, Longman, 1992.

_____. *Discourse and Social Change*. Cambridge, Polity Press, 1992.

Fisher, Louis. *Gandhi: His Life for the World*. New York: New American Library, 1982.

Forbers, Geraldine. "Women's Movement in India: Traditional Symbols and New Roles." *Social Movements in India*, ed. M.S.A. Rao. Delhi: Princeton University Press, 1979. 287-327

Foucault, Michel. *The Order of Things: An Archeology of the Human Sciences*. London and New York: Tavistock, 1970.

_____. *The Foucault Reader*, ed. Paul Rainbow. London: Penguin, 1991.

Freire, Paulo. *Pedagogy of the Oppressed*. Trans. Myra Bergman Ramos. London: Penguin, 1996.

Fuller, M.B. *The Wrongs of Indian Womanhood*. Edinburgh: Oliphant Anderson and Ferrier, 1900.

Gandhi, M.K. *An Autobiography: My Experiment with Truth*. Ahmedabad: Navajivan Publishing House, 1966.

_____. *Complete Works of Mahatma Gandhi*, Ahmedabad: Navajivan Publishing House, 1928.

_____. *Women and Social Injustice*. Ahmedabad: Navajivan Publishing House, 1954.

Gavaskar, Mahesh. "Colonialism within Colonialism: Phule's Critique of Brahmin Power." *Dalits in Modern India*, ed. S.M. Michael. Bombay: Vistaar Publication, 1990.

Gee, J.P. *Social Linguistics and Literacies: Ideology in Discourses*. London, New York, Philadelphia: Falmer Press. 1990.

Ghatak, K.K. *Hindu Revivalism in Bengal: Rammohun to Ramakrishna.*

Calcutta: Minerva Associates, 1991.

Glendon, Marg. *Rights Talk: The Impoverishment of Political Discourse,* Cambridge: Harvard University Press, 1991.

Gopal, Guru. "Dalit Women Talk Differently." *Economic and Political Weekly* 41/42 (1995).

Gosh, S.C., ed. *English Works of Rammohun Roy*, Vol. 2. Delhi: Cosmo, 1982.

Halliday, M.A.K. and R. Hasan. *Language, Context, and Text: Aspects of Language in a Social-Semiotic Perspective.* Oxford: Oxford University Press, 1985.

Hanlon, Rosalind. *Caste, Conflict and Ideology*. Hyderabad: Orient Longman, 1985.

Howarth, David. *Discourse*. New Delhi, Viva, 2002.

Iyer, Raghava. *The Moral and Political Thought of Mahatma Gandhi*. New York: Clarendon Press, 1973.

Jain, Devaki, ed. *Indian Women*. New Delhi: Ministry of Information and Broadcasting, Publications Division, 1975.

_____. "Gandhian Contributions towards a Theory of Feminist Ethic." *Speaking of Faith, Cross-Cultural Perspectives on Women, Religion and Social Change*, ed. Devaki Jain and Diana Eck. Delhi: Kali for Women, 1986.

_____. *Women's Quest for Power*. New Delhi: Vikas, 1980.

Janks, H. 'Critical discourse analysis as a research tool'. *Discourse: Studies in the Cultural Politics of Education,* London, Longman, 1997.

_____ and Ivanic, R. 'CLA and emancipatory discourse', Fairclough, ed., *Critical Language Awareness*, London, Longman, 1992.

Jatav, D.R. *Dr. Ambedkar's Role in National Movement.* New Delhi: Boudha Sahitya Sammelan, 1979.

_____. *The Social Philosophy of B.R. Ambedkar*. Agra: Phoenix, 1965.

_____. "Dr. Ambedkar's Social and Political Philosophy," *Pravartan.* Siddharth College of Arts, Science and Commerce, Golden Jubilee Commemorative Volume. Dec. 2002.

Jones, William. "The Translations of the Institutes of Manu Vide Mitakshara", B.N. Das Gupta, *Raja Rammohun Roy: The Last Phase*. New Delhi: Uppal, 1980.

Joshi, Pushpa, comp. *Gandhi on Women, Collection of Mahatma Gandhi's Writings and Speeches on Women*. Ahmedabad: Navajivan Publishing House, 1988.

Joshi, V.C., ed. *Rammohun Roy and the Progress of Modernization in India*. Delhi: Vikas Publishing House, 1975.

Kalyani, Menon-Sen and A.K. Shiva Kumar. "Women in India: How Free? How Equal?" *United Nations—India*. 2001. Web. 25th May 2009. <http://www.un.org.in/wii.htm>

Kamble, N.D. *The Scheduled Castes*. Delhi: Ashish, 1982.

Kapoor, Promilla. *Marriage and the Working Women in India.* Delhi: Vikas, 1970.

Kasibhatta, Subramanya. *Women & Law*. Hyderabad: Asia Law House, 1990.

Kaur, Amrit. *Challenge to Women*. Allahabad: New Literature, 1946.

Kaur, Inderjeet. *Status of Women in India*. Allahabad: Chug, 1983.

Keer, Dhananjay. *Dr. Ambedkar: Life and Mission*. Bombay: Popular Prakashan, 1981.

_____. *Mahatma Jyotirao Phooley: Father of the Indian Social Revolution.* 1964. Mumbai: Popular Prakashan, 2000.

Kidwai, M.H. *Women under Different Social and Religious Laws.* Delhi: Seema, 1976.

Kimmel, Michael S. "Who's Afraid of Men Doing Feminism?," from *Men Doing Feminism*, Tom Digby, ed. New York: Routledge, 1993.

King, Elizabeth Mary. *Mahatma Gandhi and Martin Luther King Jr*: the power of nonviolent action Philosophy. 1999.

Kishwar, Madhu. "Women in Gandhi" *Economics and Political Weekly*, February 20, 1988, 377-387.

_____. *Gandhi on Women*, cyclostyled paper circulated as Readings in the Women's Movement I by Bombay feminists, New Delhi: Manushi Prakashan, 1986. 56pp.

Kochar, Rajesh. *The Vedic People: Their History and Geography*. Hyderabad: Orient Longman, 2000.

Kosambi, D.D. *The Culture and Civilization of Ancient India in Historical Outline*. Delhi: Vikas, 1992.

Kumar, Radha. *The History of Doing, An Illustrated Account of Movements for Women's Rights and Feminism in India (1800-1990).* Verso Books, 1993

Lal, Shyam, et al, eds. *Ambedkar and Nation Building*. Jaipur: Rawat, 1998.

Limaye, Madhu. "B.R. Ambedkar: A Social Revolutionary." *Prime Movers: Role of the Individual in History*. New Delhi: Radiant, 1985.

Lingard, Bob and Peter Douglas. *Men engaging feminisms: Pro-feminism, backlashes and schooling*. Buckingham: England Open University Press, 1999.

Locke, Terry. *Critical Discourse Analysis*, London, Continuum Publication, 2004.

Lynch, Owen. *The Politics of Untouchability*. New York: Columbia University, 1969.

Majumdar, J.K. *Raja Ram Mohan Roy & Progressive Movement in India*. Vol. 1. Calcutta: Sadharan Brahmo Samaj, 1983.

_____, ed. *Raja Rammohun Roy and Progressive Movements in India: A Selection from Records, 1775-1845*. Calcutta: Arts Press, 1941.

Majumdar, R.C. and A.D. Pusalker, ed. *The History and Culture of the Indian People*. Volume I. Bombay: Bharatiya Vidya Bhavan, 1951.

Mani, Lata. *Contentious Traditions: The Debate on Sati in Colonial India*. Berkeley and Los Angeles: Univ. of California Press, 1998.

Manohar, K.M., ed. *Socio-Economic Status of Indian Women*. Delhi: Seema, 1983.

Merton, Thomas, ed. *Gandhi on Non-Violence*. New York: New Directions Paperback, 1964.

Michael, S.M., ed. *Dalits in Modern India*. New Delhi: Sage, 1998, 1999.

Mies, Maria. *Indian Women and Patriarchy*. New Delhi: Concept Publishing Company, 1979.

Mitter, D.N. *The Position of Women in Hindu Law*. New Delhi: Inter-India, 1984.

Moon, Vasant. *Dr. Ambedkar*. Trans. Asha Damle. New Delhi: National Book Trust, 2000.

Morton, Eleanor. *Women behind Mahatma Gandhi*. London: Max Reinhardt, 1954.

Mudbi, Baburao. "Dr. B.R. Ambedkar and the Emancipation of Indian Women," Doctoral Dissertation. University of Mysore, 1998.

Mukherjee, S.N. "The Social Implications of the Political Thought of

Raja Rammohun Roy." *Indian Society: Historical Probings*, ed. R.S. Sharma and Vivekananda Jha. Delhi: PPH, 1993.

Nag, Kalidas and Debajyoti Burman. *English Works of Raja Rammohun Roy.* Calcutta: Sadharan Brahmo Samaj, 1954.

Nanda, B.R. *Indian Women, from Purdah to Modernity*. New Delhi: Vikas, 1976.

_____. *Mahatma Gandhi: A Biography*. Oxford: O.U.P., 1958.

Nandi, Ashish. *At the Edge of Psychology: Essays in Politics and Culture.* New Delhi: Oxford University Press, 1980.

Narian, A.K. and D.C. Ahir, ed. *Dr. Ambedkar, Buddhism and Social Change*. Delhi: B.R., 1994.

Narke, Hari, ed. *Mahatma Phule: Sahitya Aur Vichar*. Bombay: Government of Maharashtra Publication, 1993.

Natrajan, S. *A Century of Social Reform in India*. Bombay: Asia, 1962.

Nurullah, Syed, and J.P. Naik. *A History of Education in India*. Bombay: Macmillan, 1951.

O'Hanlon, Rosalind. *A Comparison between Women and Men: Tarabai Shandi and the Critique of Gender Revolution in Colonial India*. New Delhi: Oxford University Press, 1994.

_____. *Caste, Conflict and Ideology: Mahatma Jyotirao Phule and Law Caste Protest in Nineteenth-Century Western India*, Cambridge: Cambridge University Press, 1985.

O'Malley, L.S.S., ed. *Modern India and the West*. New York: Oxford University Press, 1941.

Omvedt, Gail. *Cultural Revolt in a Colonial Society: The Non-Brahman Movement in Western India (1873-1930)*. Bombay: Scientific Socialist Education Trust, 1976.

_____. *Dalits and the Democratic Revolution in Colonial India.* New Delhi: Sage, 1994.

_____. *Joti Phule ani Stree-mukti ka Vichar* (Phule and Women's Liberation). Lok Vangmaya Griha, 2001.

_____. "Chhatra Yuva Sangharsh Vahini," *Aurat*, Chotanagpur Yuva Chetan Prakashan, Giridih, 1980.

Paltridge, B. *Making Sense of Discourse Analysis*. Gold Coast, Antipodean Educational Enterprises, 2000.

Parashat, Archana. *Women and Family Law Reformer in India*. Delhi: Sage, 1992.

Paradeshi, Pratima. "Ambedkar and Women's Liberation." *The Dalit,* ed. Meena Kandaswamy. Chennai: Dalit Media Network, March-April 2002. 46-49.

Parker, I. Critical Textwork: *An Introduction to Varieties of Discourse and Analysis.* Milton Keynes: Open University Press, 1999.

Patankar, Bharat and Gail Omvedt. "The Dalit Liberation Movement in Colonial Period." *Economic and Political Weekly* 14 Feb. 1979. 409-504.

Patil, P.G., trans., *Collected Works of Mahatma Jyotirao Phule.* 2 Vols. Bombay: Government of Maharashtra. 1991.

Pawar, Urmila and Meenakshi Moon. *Aamhi Itihas Ghadiwala.* Bombay: Granthali Publications, 1978.

Phillips, Louise J. and Marianne W. Jorgensen. *Discourse Analysis as Theory and Method.* London: Sage, 2002.

Phule, Jyotirao. *Collected Works of Mahatma Jyotirao Phule,* trans. P.G. Patil. 2 Vols. Bombay: Govt. of Maharashtra Publication, 1991.

_____. *Slavery,* ed. Y.D. Phadke. Mahatma Phule Source material publication: Government of Maharashtra Publication, 1990.

Pillai-Vetschera, T. *The Mahars.* New Delhi: Intercultural, 1994.

Pillai-Vetschere, T. ``Ambedkar's Daughters: A Study of Mahar Women in Ahmednagar District of Maharashtra." *Dalits in Modern India,* ed. S.M. Michael. New Delhi: Vistaar, 1999.

Rajashekharaiah, A.M. *B.R. Ambedkar—The Politics of Emancipation.* Bombay: Sindhu Publication, 1971.

Rao, M.S.A., ed. *Social Movements in India.* Delhi: Manohar, 2000.

Ray, B.N. *Reading Gandhi.* Delhi: Authors Press, 2008.

Ray, Rajat, and Sumit Sarkar. "Ram Mohun Roy and the Break with the Past." *Ram Mohun Roy and the Process of Modernization in India,* ed. V.C. Joshi. Delhi: Vikas, 1975.

Robertson, B.C. *Raja Rammohun Roy.* Delhi: O.U.P., 1999.

Roy, Ramashary. *Self and Society: A Study in Gandhian Thought.* New Delhi: Sage, 1985.

Rudolph, Lloyd, and S.H. Rudolph. *The Modernity of Tradition.* Chicago: University of Chicago Press, 1964.

Russ, Ervin Funk, "The Power of Naming: Why Men Can't Be Feminists," *Feminista!: The Journal of Feminist Construction* 1, no. 4.

Sangari, Kumkum. 'Perpetrating the Myth', *Seminar*, No. 342, Feb. 1988.

Satyamurthy, T.V., ed. *Region, Religion, Caste, Gender and Culture in Contemporary India*. Delhi: Oxford University Press, 1996.

Saxena, Kiran. *Gandhi's* Feminist Politics, Gender Equality and Patriarchal Values, www.mkgandhi-sarvodaya.org/article/kiran/20saxena.htm

Seetharamu, A.J. *Women in Organized Movements*. New Delhi: Ambika, 1981.

Sharma, R.K. *Nationalism, Social Reform and Indian Women*. Patna: Janaki Prakashan, 1981.

Shastri, Shivanath. *History of the Brahmo Samaj*. Calcutta: R. Chatterjee Publishers, 1974.

Selected Works of Rammohun Roy. New Delhi: Ministry of Information and Broadcasting, 1977.

Singh, Indu Prakash. "Dialectics of Law and the Status of Indian Women," Ph.D. thesis. Delhi: J.N.T.U, 1985.

Taneja, Anup. *Gandhi, Women and the National Movement, 1920-47*. New Delhi: Har-Anand, 2005.

Taylor, Stephanie, "Evaluating and Applying Discourse Analytical Research" in *Discourse as Data*. A Guide for Analysis, Margaret Wetherell, Stephanie Taylor and Simeon J. Yates. The Open University, London: Sage, 2001.

Teun A. Van Dijk. 'Principles of critical discourse analysis', *Discourse and Society*, 1993.

_____. *Discourse as Social Interaction*. New Delhi: Sage, Vol. 2, 1997.

_____. *Discourse as Structure and Process*. New Delhi: Sage, Vol. 1, 1997.

Thakkar, Usha. *Breaking the Shackles*: *Gandhi's Views on Women*.

Wood, Linda A and Rolf O. Kroger, *Doing Discourse Analysis*. Method for Studying Action in Talk and Text, California: Sage, 2000.

Zelliot, Eleanor. "*Dr. Ambedkar and the Mahar Movement.*" Diss: University of Pennsylvania, 1969.

_____. "The American Experience of Dr. Ambedkar's," *From Untouchables to Dalits, Essays on the Ambedkar Movement*. New Delhi: Manohar, 1992